TyING & FISHING
Soft-Hackled Nymphs

ALLEN McGEE

Frank
Amato
PORTLAND

ABOUT THE *Author*

Allen McGee has been fishing for over 30 years. He grew up bass fishing on his family's farm ponds in Northwestern Missouri. After attending college, where he majored in Journalism, he moved to the southeastern United States where he honed his fly-fishing skills fishing year round for trout on the mountain streams and tailwaters of Georgia, Tennessee, and North Carolina. He has traveled extensively fishing for trout in the northeastern United States, Midwest, and Rocky Mountain west and even as far away as the cherry trout streams of South Korea.

As a freelance outdoor writer and photographer, Allen has written articles for *Fly Fisherman* magazine and is a founding member of the fly fishing club, The International Brotherhood of the Flymph. He enjoys creating and fishing unique and innovative fly patterns that mimic not only the natural's outward appearance, but also their life stage behaviors as well. He lives with his wife in Georgia and works in television newsgathering when he's not out fishing or tying flies.

To go fishing is the chance to wash one's soul with pure air, with the rush of the brook, or with the shimmer of sun on blue water. It brings meekness and inspiration from the decency of nature, charity toward tackle-makers, patience toward fish, a mockery of profits and egos, a quieting of hate, a rejoicing that you do not have to decide a darned thing until next week. And it is discipline in the equality of men - for all men are equal before fish.

—Herbert Hoover

Published in 2007 by
FRANK AMATO PUBLICATIONS, INC.
PO Box 82112 • Portland, Oregon 97282 • (503) 653-8108
Softbound ISBN-10: 1-57188-403-3
Softbound ISBN-13: 978-1-57188-403-9
Softbound UPC: 0-81127-00237-5
Book Design: Esther Poleo
Illustrations: Loren Smith
Photography by Allen McGee
Printed in Singapore

CONTENTS

INTRODUCTION

Among the famous sayings in fishing is one that I believe to be a truism. The saying goes, "10% of anglers catch 90% of the fish". The first time I heard it I didn't really believe it, but as my fishing has taken me to many rivers and I've witnessed many fishermen in action I can confidently admit to the validity of this statement. It is my hope to share with you a strategy for catching more and larger trout. Soft-hackled nymphs and wingless wets or flymphs are the flies I have used on many occasions that I was one of the 10% of the fishermen catching 90% of the fish. An important factor that many fly-fishermen ignore is that trout feed primarily underneath the surface. It's estimated that up to 90% of a trout's diet is consumed from sub-surface food items, and the truly large fish on many streams feed exclusively under water. The reason for this is that trout are safer in their

element. The closer they get to the surface, the more risk they take as they are easier to spot by predators, including herons and osprey. This makes sub-surface feeding more energy efficient as they can feed as well as be more protected at the same time. Fish in their element are also more willing to chase after insect life because of this safety factor. Surface food items are usually more scrutinized by surface-feeding fish and energy is not put forth to chase it unless it happens to drift directly over their feeding station. Taking this into

consideration, a trout fly-fisherman should possess considerable skill in being able to use sub-surface patterns to effectively present his fly from the stream bottom to the top of the film.

The first time I learned about the flymph was in the book *The Masters on the Nymph* in the chapter written by Vernon S. Hidy. In his well-written introduction to these flies he describes the Hare's Ear and Partridge and before long this pattern became my choice fly for caddis pupae imitation. Eventually I

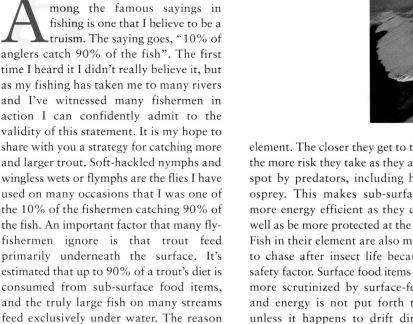

Flymph: a hatching insect between nymph and adult. A stage of metamorphosis when the insect is transforming from a wingless nymph to a fly with wings.

—Vernon Hidy, 1971

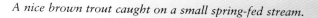

A nice brown trout caught on a small spring-fed stream.

stopped carrying conventional nymphs and instead began tying and fishing weighted and un-weighted soft-hackled nymph patterns, including flymphs, to cover the stream water column.

The Big Wood River is a classic freestone stream beginning at 8,500 feet above sea level in south central Idaho. It flows, fed by snowmelt, from the Boulder Mountains through the ski resort of Sun Valley then through agricultural fields south of Hailey into Magic Reservoir. It was on the Big Wood where I learned first-hand the effectiveness of flymphs. I had arrived at the river in early afternoon and after surveying the swift flow decided to try some traditional nymphing tactics. Soon the caddis pupae began their skyward ascent and even in the rapid water I could make out the snouts of fish breaking the surface chasing the pupae with purposeful intent. It was obvious they weren't taking adults as none were visible on the water. I looked through my fly box trying to find an imitation that would approximate the ones I couldn't see but knew were there. I had tied some pheasant-tail soft hackles, a variation on a Pheasant Tail Nymph, as I had been influenced on a flymph's effectiveness by reading Hidy's chapter in *The Masters On the Nymph* not long before this time. He had recommended the partridge and hare's ear for caddis pupae and since this pattern looked like a Hare's Ear Nymph with a partridge soft hackle I had also tied up some Pheasant Tail Nymph variations omitting the tail and using a soft-hackle collar. I cast into the current with an upstream reach mend and let the fly drift downstream, un-weighted just under the surface. As the line began to tighten and slightly belly from the influence of the current I felt a slight hesitation, a tug. Immediately I slightly lifted my rod tip to allow the hook to find a set in the cartilage of the toothy jaw. The weight of the fish combined with the current speed made for fine sport. I proceeded to catch many rainbows and a few cutthroats that afternoon. I remember working my way downstream and with every good cast that resulted in proper fly presentation I was hooking a fish. It was simply an eye-opening experience. The confidence I felt was unequalled to any fishing experience I had ever had before. As the light began to fade I had caught over twenty fish in a stretch of water not longer than fifty yards. This late-July evening on the Big Wood was where my eyes were opened to the effectiveness of the soft-hackled wingless wet fly.

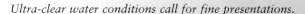

Ultra-clear water conditions call for fine presentations.

Up until this time in my fly-fishing life I had been using the same tactics I had read about over and over again in so many books and magazines. That is, use a nymph or streamer when there are no rises, then switch to dries or emergers during a hatch or spinner fall. These tactics are fundamentally sound, but restricting in many ways. They don't allow for much experimentation, but rather seem to be following a formula as if it is some sort of law. Then in the early 1990's I learned about a fly originated by Ed Story of St. Louis, Missouri called the Crackleback. The Crackleback is a "Dry Woolly" based

on the well-known wet-fly Woolly Worm pattern. As It is intended to be both a dry fly and a wet fly and can be fished from the stream bottom to the surface equally effectively. Wooly Worms are often fished with traditional wet fly tactics and the Crackleback, when swung downstream, can be fished similarly. Tying and fishing the Crackleback in a No.10 or a No.12 exclusively, Ed's been fishing this fly and its variations since inventing the pattern in the early 1950's and even patterns the logo of his fly-fishing mail-order catalogs after the Crackleback. I tied some of Ed's flies and began to fish them in the way he described.

The presentation calls for casting up or across stream, fishing the fly initially as a dry fly. As the fly drifts across and downstream past the angler drag begins and is used along with a line tug to pull the fly under water, fishing it through the downstream swing as a sub-surface imitation with a skipping action imparted with the rod tip. Fished sub-surface, the Crackleback has similarities with a flymph or fished more deeply a soft-hackled nymph. As I fished often with Crackleback's I found strikes were frequently violent at the end of the drift when the fly was swinging or even when the drift was over and the fly was hanging in the current below me. Ed's advice was to let the fly hang in the current below for about twenty seconds before stripping the fly back. And he was right; I caught many fish when the Crackleback was just hanging in the current below me. It must have been so tempting to see food just sitting there that the trout finally smashed it. Fish would also quite often strike when the fly was stripped across-current or back towards my casting position as well. By using these presentations I was employing some of the same techniques that are used with soft-hackle nymphs and wingless wets, as well as learning skills of presentation and fly manipulation that have been used for ages with wet flies.

I then started tying a variation of Ed's Crackleback that I named the Q-Back. It's basically the same profile design except for material selection. The fly is tied with a sparse peacock herl body, oversized barred ginger saddle hackle, and a red thread head. There was a time period that I fished the Q-Back in a size 12 almost exclusively every time I fished. I carried a box full of them and by not having to think about which fly I was going to use I really began to concentrate more on trout behavior and fly presentation. It tuned me in to the fact that if a fly looks naturally alive and appears to be something good to eat many times the fish will not care if it's something he hasn't seen before. The important part lies in your presentation of the fly and allowing yourself to be invisible to the fish. I fished the No.12 Q-back pattern for nearly two years only rarely changing to a No.16 or a No.20 Q-back over the course of this time period and I caught more fish on a daily basis than before I had learned about Ed Story's Crackleback and its fishing methods. It was not too long after this that I started tying and using traditional English soft-hackle wet-fly patterns made famous by the North Country School of fly-fishermen. From there I then began adapting all my nymphs to have a soft-hackle collar turning them into soft-hackled nymphs and flymphs.

The flies presented here will allow you to match any mayfly nymph or caddis pupae. In addition, I am presenting patterns and techniques to imitate midge, scuds, and stoneflies. The new patterns utilize the best of today's material choices. The design of these soft-hackled flies allows for variation of the body and hackle color shades to match the naturals' body and wing colors. Not all of the patterns presented here fit the traditional definitions of flymphs or wingless wet flies, however the ideas behind them and inspiration for them came significantly from the work of James Leisenring and Vernon "Pete" Hidy. More important to my confidence in them were the many days spent on the water seeing how fish reacted to the soft-hackled nymph and flymph imitations, and allowing the fish to guide me in coming up with ideas for my own flies.

Something fascinating happens to a fly pattern when you wrap a game-bird feather around the hook. The fly suddenly comes to life not only at your vise, but more importantly in the water as well. When I get to a river I will first survey the stream and weather conditions. Then I read the water. This information is vital and helps me choose the correct fly. Only then do I open the fly box and pick the correct size, shape, color, and weight fly pattern. Most of the time a soft-hackled nymph or flymph is the first and only fly I need to tie on. Even in the relatively rare surface-feeding periods using a flymph to imitate the emergers is my first choice. At times I use traditional dry flies if I want to imitate fully formed upright-winged adult mayflies (possibly spinners) or terrestrials, but I have such confidence in soft-hackled nymphs to catch fish that I use them to cover practically every important streamborn invertebrate life stage.

In this book I will cover the traditional tying and fishing techniques as conceived by G.E.M. Skues, Frank Sawyer, James Leisenring and Vernon Hidy. I am also going to present new fly-tying design options and uses for soft-hackled nymphs and wingless wet flies. Whereas these flies were originally most often designed to imitate emerging mayfly and caddisfly naturals they can also be tied to imitate midge pupae, scuds, and stonefly nymphs, as well as egg-laying stages of mayflies and caddisflies. I have taken the design ideas behind the success of the original soft-hackled wet flies and fishing methods, the mimicry of the living insect, and expanded it to include imitations of the most important food items found in trout streams. Please join me in discovering how these flies can be used to imitate specific life stages of trout-stream naturals. These soft-hackled wingless wet flies deserve the recognition they have earned because they are so very effective.

—Allen McGee
September 2005

Soft-hackled nymphs are good anytime, anywhere fly patterns.

Chapter One

HISTORY OF
The Soft-Hackled Nymph

Honey Dun.

Many of today's nymph and pupae patterns are tied so realistically that while imitating very specific mayfly and caddisfly species on the tying bench, they don't fish near as well as they look. The soft-hackled patterns presented here have ancient origins yet will often out-fish many of the more modern artificials. The bugginess and impression of life these patterns elicit prove irresistible to trout when presented in the correct manner. Wingless wet fly, flymph, soft hackle, soft-hackle thorax nymph, North Country Spider, soft-hackled wet fly, the names that these flies are known by are numerous however they all are related to each other in one way or another. The common theme is that all of these flies have soft bird-feather hackle collars, the movement of which makes them incredibly attractive to fish. The flies may have been invented at different times or fished in varying manners, however the bottom line is that they have the same concept of movement tied into their pattern. The biggest difference among the intended uses of these patterns is the depth at which they are traditionally fished. The earliest soft hackles, such as the North Country Spiders, are very sparse patterns intended to be fished in the film or on top the water as emergers or adults. As the soft-hackle fly progressed over time, the depth at which it was fished became deeper. This was a slow process as the geographical area near where these flies were created, specifically southern England, held anglers that believed the only civilized and sporting way in which to fish for trout was with a high-floating, adult fly pattern, i.e. dry-fly tactics. The knowledge of trout feeding behavior eventually led anglers into discovering that nymph fishing was day in and day out a more productive approach to catching trout, especially on the freestone streams where insect hatches and surface feeding is less common than on the chalkstreams. The road that has led to modern nymph fishing was by way of winged wet-fly fishing. Between these two periods many talented and influential anglers, including G.E.M. Skues and James Leisenring, found that they had more success with a wingless wet-fly pattern and these are the flies this book will concentrate on. The wingless wet fly or the flymph is a transitional emerger pattern fished from inches under the surface up to the top while the soft-hackled nymph covers deeper water from the stream bottom up to where the flymph takes over. Both flymphs and the soft-hackled nymphs are overlooked and underfished flies that when tied and presented correctly can be the most versatile fly patterns ever created.

Soft-hackled nymphs are used to imitate the nymphal stage of aquatic insects, including the mayfly, caddisfly, and stonefly species. The soft-hackle collared fly concep thas been around for over five hundred years but in order to know what the fish find the soft-hackle collar to specifically represent you'd have to ask them. Many anglers feel that it replicates the naturals' legs, and in the case of flymphs the emerging wings. But one thing is for sure, the soft-hackle fibers convey movement which in turn suggests life. The main requirement is that they have soft hackle bird feathers and no wing, unlike the traditional wet flies. Soft-hackled nymphs are designed to be fished on the bottom of the stream or near it in the same fashion as today's nymphs. The benefits are that soft-hackle nymphs have much more life to them than most modern nymph patterns and can be fished not only dead-drifted, but also with action imparted by the angler or the current.

A flymph can best be defined as a fly in a state of transformation from its nymphal stage to a winged adult. Flymphs will be discussed as being the artificials that are fished from feet below up to the top of the surface film, whatever is necessary to present the fly to a potential trout.

Pete Hidy coined the term "flymph" to better describe the wingless wet fly as used to imitate emerging caddisfly pupae and mayfly nymphs. Hidy actually got the name flymph from the wingless hackle wet flies that his friend James Leisenring tied feeling that "flymph" was a better term for these flies as they were used to represent what are considered emergers - the transitional stage between the nymph and the adult. I believe that Hidy came up with the term flymph because he wanted to name the patterns so people could associate them with a specific stage of fly imitation whereas the term wingless wet fly or spider doesn't specifically describe the life stage is being imitated. There are few presentation and casting differences between the shn's and flymphs but which fly and under what conditions it is used depends on the life stage of the insect you are trying to duplicate. Fish love soft-hackled nymphs and flymphs and between them you can cover the stream from the bottom to the top.

What exactly are the differences between soft hackled spiders and flymphs? I consider spiders, i.e. traditional soft hackles, to be flies that are fished in or immediately under the surface film and shn's (soft-hackled nymphs) are flies fished on or near the stream bottom. Flymphs are transitional sub-surface flies filling the niche between the soft-hackled nymph and the spider or the dry fly. While flymphs borrow the concept of using a soft-hackle collar from the spiders they separate themselves in their identity by their fuller, buggier, and quite often translucent spun fur bodies that emphasizes the hydrofuge of air bubbles that natural emerging mayflies, caddisflies, and midge exhibit. Furthermore, flymphs are not necessarily

Pale Watery Dun Wingless.

Iron Blue Dun Flymph.

defined by their body materials but as an approach to fly fishing. That is the flymph is a transitional ascending fly pattern, one that is fished with specific methods that activate the flies bodies and hackle collars bringing them to life and mimicking the naturals in both appearance and behavior.

The term flymph is also a descriptive noun. For instance, a Pheasant Tail Flymph is recognizable as a fly that is fished as an emerger employing characteristics of both the traditional Pheasant Tail nymph with the addition of a soft hackle collar, but there's more to it because it's understood that since it's called a flymph it should be fished in a manner that will activate the soft-hackle collar and allow the fly to rise naturally up through the water column, i.e. with an up and across stream cast to allow the fly to

surface. The combination of a translucent, buggy fur body and a pulsating hackle bring these flies to life and the manner in which they are fished, down and across, under water. rising to the surface is every bit as important as their construction. We have to understand this integral relationship between fly construction and the presentation that activates these flies, bringing them to life, to truly understand the concepts lay forth by Leisenring and Hidy and influenced by Skues, Stewart and others before them.

Hidy used the term "mimicry flymphs" to describe wingless wet flies that carry an air bubble hydrofuge similar to that which many aquatic insect carry on their bodies as they rise to the surface. These air bubbles are created when the nymphal shuck is split open and the insect be it a

very similar to this profile. According to Hidy, "Color, Undercolor, Natural Color Harmony, Translucence, Texture, Size, Shape, Proportions, Delicacy, and Vitality" are the characteristics that need to be imitated in artificial flies. Adding mimicry is the attempt of simulating life in the flies through appearance, movement, and behavior thus hopefully making them appear more realistic to the fish so that they are fully confident in taking our flies. A translucent tapered body created by spinning fur on silk and wrapping a hackle collar simulates the life-like properties of the natural.

Many fishermen use a host of fly patterns to imitate every stage of the immature or emerging mayfly, caddisfly, and midge pupae. However, the fact is that apart from size, these immature insects look loosely similar to each before they hatch into adults, particularly as they are crawling out of their nymphal shucks.

Frank Sawyer wrote this about imitating swimmer-type mayfly nymphs, "Since I started fishing with the nymph I have evolved patterns to imitate all members of this swimming group and, indeed, had success with them. But I found there was no need for any exact likeness of one or another and that if most of the details and characteristics of several could be incorporated in two patterns the fish could be taken consistently on them. General shape and coloration, together with the right size, is of greater importance than an exact copy." Sawyer in fact only used two patterns to imitate the mayfly nymphs in the chalkstreams of southern England, the Pheasant Tail for the darker nymphs and the Grey Goose for the lighter nymphs. Sawyer felt that aside from the impressionistic characteristics of the nymph the most important factor in catching trout was to "have confidence in your ability to make your artificial look and behave like a natural." It is with this in mind that I hope to be able to show the reader how both soft-hackled nymphs and flymphs can so successfully represent the immature stages of trout-stream aquatic insects. These flies take us beyond size, shape, and color in matching the naturals. We must bring life to our patterns and one way to do this is to try to imitate movement as well. It's one of the triggers fish find attractive and use to key in on their prey.

Both soft-hackled nymphs and wingless wets fulfill another requirement

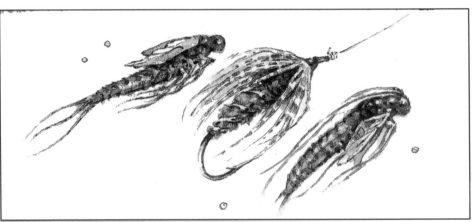

When the natural mayfly nymphs and caddis pupae are rising to the surface they look similar with legs held tight to the body for an aerodynamic ascent. Their behavior and ability to move in the water however is quite different dependent upon the species and you need to match this behavior correctly as well as the size, shape, and color of the natural. A correctly colored flymph fished with the appropriate action will be very effective in imitating both mayfly and caddis emergers.

sink below the intended target level and then fished down and across possibly with added line mends to let the fly swing naturally and rise to the surface. Thus a fly that has a soft hackle collar and a buggy body fished in a manner intended to imitate emerging invertebrates under the water surface is then considered a fly/nymph or flymph.

While it sometimes is, a flymph doesn't have to be categorized based on it's body, hackle, hook, or any other characteristics of it's construction other than it's a type of wingless wet fly intended to imitate emerging invertebrates in the most vulnerable, enticing, and available stage to the trout – under water., not on the

mayfly, caddisfly, or midge is crawling out while unfolding its wings.

Trout love an easy meal often keying in on emergers or stillborns inches under the surface film. We as trout fisherman would be wise to concentrate on fishing artificials that imitate these vulnerable stages. Flymphs do a fantastic job of imitating a very vulnerable stage in the life cycle of aquatic insects, imitating a fly that is crawling out of its nymphal shuck with the soft hackle fibers simulating legs and wing pads struggling to free themselves. Natural emerging mayfly and caddis pupae hold their legs swept back against their bodies as they are rising during emergence. The soft hackle fibers on the flymph patterns look that I find important. They meet all the definitions of what makes a great fly. First they are quick and easy to tie. This makes them fun to tie as well. They can be tied anywhere, as they require few materials. The materials are both easily obtainable and can be found in any fly shop whether it's close to home or near a distant river. Above all, these flies allow for experimental input from the tier resulting in limitless design variation options to match the local insect species.

In order to trace the history and find the origin of the soft-hackled nymph we must look at the recorded documentation of the soft-hackle wet fly. The earliest written description of a fly that we would recognize as a soft hackle can be found in one of the first books on fly fishing itself. Dame Juliana Berner is thought to have been the abbess of a Benedictine Nunnery in Sopwell located in southeastern England outside of London. In 1425, she wrote the book entitled *The Book of St. Albains*. It was distributed by hand copies made by monks for fifty years until it was finally printed in 1496. This writing intended for the nobles and gentlemen, contained information describing the great arts of the day such as hunting and heraldry. It also included an article entitled The Treatyse of Fysshynge wyth an Angle which is thought to be the first English literary work detailing fly fishing. The article is a detailed observation of hatching flies and trout feeding behavior. In it were descriptions of twelve flies one for each month of the year to match the conditions encountered on the stream. One of these is called the "donne fly". The description being 'the body of donne woll and the wyngis of the partryche' has been thought to be the fly known as the Partridge & Orange, a fly that is still fished today. This work was instrumental in the history of fly fishing and introduced it as a higher art form for the upper class.

James Chetham of Smedley anonymously published The Angler's Vade Mecum in 1681. The book was later enlarged and re-printed in 1689. In reference to North Country spiders Chetam wrote about the use of game birds for hackle collars instead of only poultry feathers and while many of his fly pattern were winged wet flies he also listed some familiar North Country spider recipes. Chetam may also have been the first to write about spinning fur on silk to form fly bodies where an undercolor of silk would

The importance of sparseness in the Partridge & Orange cannot be over-emphasized.

show the fur creating the translucent body effect many aquatic insects have.

As we are solely discussing soft-hackles we will skip ahead in time into the 1800's where much was written about these flies. It was in the 1800's that these flies began to be classified and well documented. They earned the name North Country flies as a reference to the north of England on the border of Scotland where the soft-hackled wet fly was invented and fished.

In 1857, W.C. Stewart's *The Practical Angler* came out. This work is considered important as it is evident that Stewart was ahead of his time in both his knowledge of trout behavior and stream approach. He fished his soft-hackle patterns using upstream dry-fly methods both to achieve a natural float and to keep his presence concealed. Stewart is best known for introducing us to his palmered spiders presenting directions for tying and fishing three of these flies: the Dun Spider, the Black Spider, and the Red Spider. These flies are tied very sparse with the body consisting of only silk thread on top of which the hackle is palmered from the

center of the hook shank up to the hook eye. The three palmered sections represent the three thoracic leg segments of the natural insects and the colors they are tied in imitate the most commonly found trout-stream aquatic insects. The sparseness of these patterns belies their effectiveness. Stewart fished these flies using an upstream presentation casting across and above the fish while stressing the importance of allowing the fly to drift naturally in the currents devoid of drag. This strategic approach of positioning himself before making the cast related his knowledge of the importance of presentation and allowing the fish to only see the fly while the angler should remain invisible. Spiders are still effectively fished today and although Stewart didn't fish these patterns as sub-surface flies, they had a great deal of influence on later anglers who modified them for deeper fishing.

John Swarbrick was an angler who farmed in Ilkley, a town in Yorkshire, England. In 1807, drawing on a variety of sources, he compiled a list of traditional soft-hackled flies. The list was added to in

Standard Collar Hackle.

Tail-less.

STYLES
OF *Flymphs*

Palmered Hackle.

1890 with additions from J.W. Sagar. It wasn't until 1907 that the pamphlet "A List of Wharfedale Flies" was printed with the effort of E. Beanlands and a local Yorkshire printer. Among the flies listed in the writing are the March Brown, Partridge, Dark Bloe, Light Bloe, and Grey Midge. In addition to these there were other patterns listed as well, all of which are similar to patterns that are still used. The title of the pamphlet refers to the River Wharfe, a northern English brown trout stream that flows through Yorkshire and that was fished by these men as their local water. The patterns listed in this pamphlet would go on to be known as North Country flies and became famous in the works of Pritt, Lee, Edmunds, Jackson and others.

The North Country flies were originally developed to be fished in fast-water highland streams that had few rises from trout. Northern streams were generally freestone, more turbulent and less fertile than the chalkstreams, and the anglers who fished them needed to resort to different tactics other than dry flies because the trout didn't rise as freely as on the more placid spring creeks to the south. Out of necessity, the North Country flies were invented to be fished in the surface film or just under the surface. As a result, anglers were discovering that more fish could be caught by fishing their flies deeper because the fish were conditioned to finding their food sub-surface. The defining characteristic of these patterns is their sparseness. Their bodies were not of fur but of silk floss, sometimes with a fur thorax, wire ribbing, and a very sparse turn of soft hackle. The success of these flies was impressive. These patterns did a wonderful job of imitating emerging nymphs, stillborn adults, or even drowned mayflies. The soft-hackle spiders were fished upstream with line held off the water using a long rod to avoid drag. The dry-fly purists of southern England however were not taken with the idea of a fly that didn't imitate the fully emerged adult and avoided using spiders even though they were out-fished by the northern anglers. The anglers who fished the soft hackles were known as the North Country school and it took a while before the popularity of their patterns spread. Up until this time, fishing winged wet flies had been the preferred method if there wasn't a hatch coming off and fish rising. These particular wet flies had enough success to merit their popularity, however the question of which life stage of the natural they represented was enough to drive some angler's in search of better fly design.

Throughout the 1800's the soft-hackle spiders continued to gain popularity. Some of the most important books on the flies were written in the mid and late 19th century. A few of these important titles include Alfred Ronalds' *A Fly Fisher's Entomology* 1849, H. C. Cutcliffe *The Art of Trout Fishing in Rapid Streams* 1863, William Blacker *Art of Fly Making* 1855, Francis Francis *A Book on Angling* 1867, T.E. Pritt *Yorkshire Flies* 1885 and *North Country Flies* 1886, and in 1916 H.H. Edmonds and N.N. Lee's *Brook and River Trouting*. These works can be considered essential in introducing anglers to the soft-hackle wet flies. Of these angling authors, Pritt and Edmonds and Lee are considered the fathers of the soft-hackled wet fly.

Thomas Evan Pritt was the angling editor of the *Yorkshire Post* however he is known for his books that described many of the North Country flies still in use today. The book *Yorkshire Flies* was first published in 1885 and limited to 200 copies. In 1886 it was re-published in greater numbers and became available to more anglers. In this book Pritt discusses how soft hackles are an improvement over the winged wet fly saying, "It is now conceded that a fly dressed hacklewise is generally to be preferred to a winged imitation... Trout undoubtedly take a hackled fly for the insect just rising from the pupae in a half-drowned state; and the opening and closing of the fibres of the feathers give it an appearance of vitality, which even the most dextrous fly-fisher will fail to impart to the winged imitation."

Some of the patterns Pritt describes are the Partridge & Orange, Olive Bloa, Greenwell's Spider, Dark Snipe and Purple, Grey Gnat, Starling Bloa, Water Cricket, Little Black, Waterhen Bloa, and the Grey Partridge. The beauty of these patterns is that when wet the body materials, particularly the ones tied with silk, take on a darker yet semi-transparent color that is similar to the naturals while the soft-hackle collars imitate legs and wings. For example, the orange silk in the Partridge & Orange becomes a light brown imitating many mayfly nymph color shades.

Another landmark work is considered to be Edmonds and Lee's *Brook and River Trouting* published in 1916.

This book contains some of the same patterns as Pritt's *Yorkshire Flies* but it also introduced some new ones for imitating sedge, such as the Light Sedge, Dark Sedge, Light Silverhorns, and Dark Silverhorns. The authors also get more specific about imitation by describing the natural that each fly was designed to imitate.

While the soft-hackle flies up to this point had been used for fishing on the surface or just under the surface, the biggest influence on wet flies used when fishing the entire water column came from G.E.M. Skues. This man did more for nymph fishing than any fisherman that came before him. George Edward MacKenzie Skues was born in 1858 and his contributions to the sport of fly fishing, particularly nymphing, cannot be overstated. Skues was a lawyer and a solitary bachelor which gave him ample time to spend fishing for and observing trout. He lived in Hampshire, England and fished the Itchen, in particular, a section known as Abbots Barton which is a network of local springs creating numerous small chalkstreams and watery meadows.

Blue Dun.

Skues spent 57 years fishing this specific area and knew the Itchen and its trout like no other. He went against the prevalent ideas of his contemporaries, many of whom were members of the Flyfishers' Club of London and felt that the only way to catch trout was on the surface using a dry fly. Undeterred by their criticism, Skues went quietly about observing fish and perfecting his nymphing strategies.

In his first book *Minor Tactics of the Chalk Stream,* written in 1910, Skues introduced fishing upright-winged adult wet flies under the surface. For this he was seen as a rule breaker by his fellow anglers. While this book didn't talk about the nymphs as we know them today, he was fishing basically dry flies tied with materials that made them sink, it did break new ground in the angling community as all the southern chalkstream fishermen strictly fished only on the surface of the stream. Skues early sub-surface patterns were adult flies, essentially upright-winged wet flies fished upstream using a drag-free float. The book was titled *Minor Tactics* as a sign of respect shown for the dry-fly elitist club members, however much Skues felt that sub-

Skues' soft-hackled thorax nymphs.

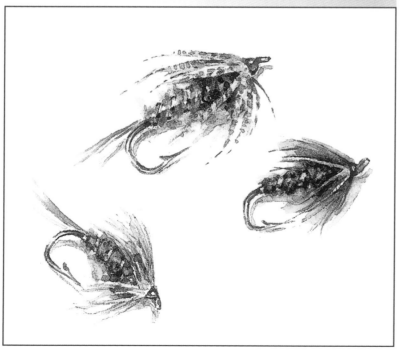

Gray Hackle.

surface fishing was important. He even dedicated the book to the "dry fly purist". However, this was the last time he apologized to his fellow anglers, for in 1921, Skues wrote *The Way of a Trout with a Fly*. In this book Skues moves away from the adult winged wet-fly patterns into a more realistic nymph representation and approach to the sub-surface naturals. He found that the best natural nymph imitations were wingless wet flies tied with soft-hackle collars. In doing so he named his new patterns soft-hackled thorax nymphs. This was the first time the word "nymph" was used for a fly pattern. These nymph patterns were very similar to the ones that James Leisenring would later use and are also similar to many patterns still used today. Skues' nymphs were tied with hen soft-hackle collars defined by a dominant thorax of fur tapering down to a sparse abdomen of either peacock herl, fur dubbing or quill, and ending with hen hackle tailing fibers.

Not only were Skues' nymph patterns a revolution, but so too was his approach to observing the naturals. Through careful insect sampling he studied and matched his nymphs to those he found in the Itchen. He then tied his flies to imitate the naturals in size, shape, and color and, equally as important, fished them with natural presentations that were similar to the swimming mayflies' behavior.

G.E.M. Skues went on to write *Nymph Fishing for Chalk Stream Trout* in 1939. This book summed up his approach to nymph fishing which in essence was that since trout feed primarily under water, by matching the natural mayfly nymph as closely as possible and then fishing the fly with life mimicking behaviors, the fish would strike. Slight sub-surface drag or movement, Skues contended, can actually be attractive if not too extreme as it is an indication of life in the artificial, an idea that many anglers such as Leisenring, Hidy, Sawyer, and Kite, would expand upon. Skues was a major influence on Jim Leisenring and the two corresponded through letters before Skues' death in 1949.

After Skues, nymph fishing slowly began to gain acceptance with anglers. However many club waters in southern England still have strict rules on fishing presentation and fly usage. Some don't allow sub-surface fishing or, if they do, the fly must be fished upstream. Nonetheless many fishermen began to use nymph patterns and found out first-hand the importance of the nymph to the trout's diet. As more knowledge of the sub-surface feeding patterns of trout came to light, and fly fishermen used these new techniques, a whole new world opened up to the angler. One that didn't rely on hatches or opportunistic surface feeding to catch trout but instead took the fly directly to the fish.

Born in 1878, James E. Leisenring was a native-born Pennsylvanian from Seidersville, near Allentown. Standing over 6 feet tall, and known to his friends as "Big Jim," he was a true Pennsylvania Dutchman. Fishing was a way of life for Leisenring. From 1910 to 1940, while studying Skues and Stewart's works, he was continually evolving his own fly patterns and fishing techniques. In 1941 he published *The Art of Tying the Wet Fly* which is now considered the landmark work on these flies. This is mainly a fly-tying book that outlined his favorite wet-fly patterns for deceiving trout. He placed a great amount of importance on how the fly appeared to eyes of the fish. One of the ways he imitated the naturals was by using spun fur dubbed bodies and silk thread thus creating a wet-fly that simulated the translucent nymph. The soft-hackle collar too added a lifelike quality to the flies and when fished using his techniques the fly became alive or "deadly" as Leisenring would say. In his book he describes one of his fishing techniques, in an all too brief chapter, a method that is now known as the Leisenring Lift. This presentation method is a form of induced take made by lifting the rod tip as the fly appears in front of the fish which animates the fibers of the soft-hackle and triggers a feeding strike. Leisenring worked out these methods on the Little Lehigh and Broadhead Creek where he was infamous for taking large numbers of fish. Other anglers longed to know his secrets. In fact Leisenring was so good that even Skues couldn't help but sing his praises among the British anglers. While relatively well known in the United States at this time he was more recognized for his talents by the English anglers as Skues had presented Leisenring's flies and techniques to the Fly Fisher's Club of London. One reason that Leisenring isn't more well known to anglers is that his book was written during World War II when the minds of many were focused on winning the war. The knowledge of Leisenring's importance to wet-fly fishing has increased since that time but there are still many who

James Leisenring.

*From **THE ART OF TYING THE WET FLY & FISHING THE FLYMPH** by James E. Leisenring and Vernon S. Hidy, copyright 1971 by Vernon S. Hidy. Used by permission of Crown Publishers, a division of Random House, Inc.

Photo courtesy Crown Publishers

can learn from his strategies.

Leisenring is often referred to as "The American Skues" so influential were his wet-fly skills. Written under the title of the 1941 edition of *The Art of Tying the Wet Fly* it reads "by Jim Leisenring as told to Pete Hidy". Vernon "Pete" Hidy was a young pupil of Leisenring's who helped in the writing of this book and who was an excellent angler in his own right. Hidy went on to write three new chapters in the 1971 revised edition of *The Art of Tying the Wet Fly and Fishing the Flymph*. Other students of Leisenring included Dick Clark and Chip Stauffer who taught Leisenring's tactics to many anglers, including Art Flick who learned and fished them on Schoharie Creek in the New York Catskills. Leisenring continued fishing and refining his skills on Broadhead Creek in Pennsylvania until his death in 1951.

In the same year John Atherton wrote *The Fly and the Fish*. This book was one of the first to discuss the wet-fly being used to imitate emergers. Atherton wrote, "It is quite possible that wet-fly fishing and dry-fly fishing shade into one another on occasion, the dividing line being indiscernible." Atherton's book investigates tying flies in a way that gives the fish an impression of each of the life stages of the natural.

In the 1950's, anglers really began noting trout behavior and insect study. Many influential and enlightening books on nymph fishing were written in this decade. Among these was Frank Sawyer's first book *Keeper of the Stream* in 1952 and *Nymphs and the Trout* in 1958. In these books, Sawyer demonstrates his angling ability with fishing nymphs. Frank Sawyer became a riverkeeper on the Avon River in Wiltshire, England when he was eighteen. Over the years he developed many new nymphing practices and flies that are still widely used today. One famous method still utilized today is the "induced take". Sawyer approached fly fishing beyond the point of view of the angler, with trying to think like fish and to use techniques that the fish would find attractive. After years of experimentation he found out he needed only two nymph fly patterns, tied in different sizes and both of his own invention, the Pheasant Tail and the Grey Goose, describing them as his "universal patterns". In fact, not only were the number of different patterns Sawyer carried minimal so were the design and materials used. The original Pheasant Tail Nymph is a hook, copper wire, and pheasant-tail fibers. The Grey Goose consists of a hook, gold wire, and gray goose-wing wing herl. Both patterns are tied with the same profile. Sawyer tied these flies in three sizes and was able to imitate any mayfly nymph in the Avon or many other streams with them. Of this

Avon River.

minimal fly approach Sawyer writes, "Confidence in what you have to offer goes a long way to success, but, even more, you need to have confidence in your ability to make your artificial look and behave like a natural."

Oliver Kite was a pupil of Frank Sawyer and learned many of his skills from the master. He was an expert in chalkstream nymph fishing and felt that in clear-water streams nymph patterns should be kept realistic through minimal dressings. Kite is recognized as being one of the greatest clear-water or Netheravon-style, nymph fishermen. The term Netheravon comes from the name of a village on the River Avon where both Frank Sawyer and Oliver Kite lived. Kite, like his mentor Sawyer, not only thought like an angler but also like a fish. He would approach the water thinking from the fish's point of view, analyzing the currents, food supply, water conditions, and feeding lies before choosing the appropriate fly to meet these criteria. Oliver Kite wrote Nymph Fishing in Practice in 1963. This book contains many nymph techniques including the "induced take" that Frank Sawyer had invented. Kite, like Sawyer, felt the nymph had to look alive in the water. "Successful nymph fishing is primarily dependent on the life-like employment of the artificial by the angler," he wrote.

Vernon S. Hidy was born in 1914 in Ohio and moved to Pennsylvania after college. "Pete" as he was known by his friends, had been refining his skills in the streams of the Pocono and Catskill mountains when he met his soon-to-be-mentor James Leisenring on Broadhead Creek while both were fishing. According to Hidy, Leisenring didn't even notice him because he was so focused on playing a trout that had just taken one of his wet flies. Hidy would later convince Leisenring to write a book about his "deadly" fly-tying and fishing techniques. With Pete Hidy's help Jim Leisenring wrote the seminal work The Art of Fishing the Wet Fly in 1941. Hidy also knew Reuben Cross and Harry and Elsie Darbee, anglers who all shared their fly-fishing knowledge with him. After serving in the Navy in World War II, Pete and his wife Elaine moved to Oregon where he found fabulous trout fishing that he captured in his photographs.

Out West he came into his own as an angling writer beginning with Sports Illustrated Fly Fishing in 1960, which was revised and re-printed in 1972, and then The Pleasures of Fly Fishing in 1972, a beautifully photographed book that related Hidy's affection for trout streams. In addition, Pete Hidy wrote two articles on the flymph for Fly-Fisherman magazine in 1971. The Pleasures of Fly Fishing contains photographs of some of the great western trout streams, including Silver Creek. He had since moved to Boise, Idaho and had the opportunity to test his flymphs on some of the most selective spring-creek trout in the world. In 1971 he co-authored the revised version of The Art

Sawyer Pheasant Tail Nymph.

of Tying the Wet Fly and Fishing the Flymph. This was the original 1941 book by Leisenring, with a second part added. Part II of The Art of Tying the Wet Fly and Fishing the Flymph contained three new chapters on wingless wet-fly patterns introducing Hidy's use of the term "flymph". The flymph was a specific name given to a soft-hackled wingless wet-fly used to imitate emerging mayfly nymphs or caddis pupae. Hidy's definiton of a flymph: "a wingless artificial fly with a soft, translucent body of fur or wool which blends with the undercolor of the tying silk when wet, utilizing soft-hackle fibers easily activated by currents to give the effect of an insect alive in the water,

and strategically cast diagonally upstream or across for the trout to take just below or within a few inches of the surface film".

A flymph or wingless wet is a particular pattern meant to be fished in the few inches of water up to the surface and that imitates emergers. He cites Ernest Schwiebert as the "first angler, to my knowledge, to specify a dressing for an insect at the moment of its emergence" when in Matching the Hatch Schwiebert had specified that a 'wet-fly subimago pattern imitated the emerging March Browns.' Schwiebert's discussion in this book focuses on specific patterns for imitating mayfly, caddis, and midge from an entomological viewpoint.

Another influence on Hidy's confirmation of the importance of using wet flies to imitate emerging insects was Art Flick. In The New Streamside Guide Flick offered that "just prior to emergence mayfly nymphs are most active" and Flick suggests using un-weighted Hendrickson nymphs, for example, fished with dry-fly tactics to match the hatch during the emergence. Hidy summed up his fishing philosophy with the chapter entitled "Soft-hackle Nymphs-the Flymphs" in the book The Masters on the Nymph, 1979 which

Vernon "Pete" Hidy

*From **THE ART OF TYING THE WET FLY & FISHING THE FLYMPH** by James E. Leisenring and Vernon S. Hidy, copyright 1971 by Vernon S. Hidy. Used by permission of Crown Publishers, a division of Random House, Inc.

popular nymphs of all time. Dave states that the RFSH nymph is the single most important fly he carries and is responsible for catching more trout, whitefish, and char, both in terms of size and quantity, than any other fly he has ever fished. Its effectiveness is due to the dubbing combination of the orange shade abdomen and darker thorax red-fox fur being blended with Antron to produce an eye-catching shimmer, as well as holding tiny air bubbles that reflect light. The long, spiky squirrel-hair fibers, and the addition of the soft-hackled collar tied with either partridge, grouse or hen portray moving gills and legs, suggesting movement and life, making the RFSH irresistible to fish.

Another modern soft-hackled nymph pattern is Hump's Sulphur Nymph created by Joe Humphreys. This is a two-tone fur nymph with an orangish-yellow abdomen, a brown thorax and a mottled brown hen soft-hackle collar tied short with the hackle tips only extending to the hook point like a thorax nymph.

Having begun using glass beads tied into flies around 1900, Italian fly fishermen have long known the advantages of using beads to weight a wet fly to achieve a faster sink rate

In the late 1970's, Roman Moser adapted this idea to include using metal beads for weighting his nymphs, an idea which is now a very popular method and can be used effectively in the soft-hackled nymphs.

The important works by the anglers presented here are a "milestone history" of the soft-hackled nymphs and the wingless wets "flymphs", a history that will continue to be written by generations of anglers that continue to tie new soft-hackled nymph patterns.

included alonside chapters written by some of the greatest fly fishermen in the world, Frank Sawyer, Ernest Schwiebert, Al Troth, and Charles Brooks among others. Pete Hidy passed away in 1983 in Boise, Idaho leaving the angling world with writings that express his love of trout streams and beautiful flies. He had a direct link to some of the greatest anglers in history. His on-stream observations that accompanied his fishing techniques and soft-hackled wet-fly patterns displayed a keen angling knowledge.

One of the more recent soft-hackled nymphs is Cal Bird's Bird's Nest. Originally invented in 1959 to fish the Truckee River, this fly has become a standard nymph pattern across the country. The Bird's Nest is versatile and makes a very successful emerging caddis pupae, a diving egg-laying caddis, and also a general-purpose nymph for prospecting. The mallard flank collar and tail prove enticing to trout.

In 1966, Dave Whitlock invented the Red Fox Squirrel-Hair Nymph. This fly still remains one of the most effective and

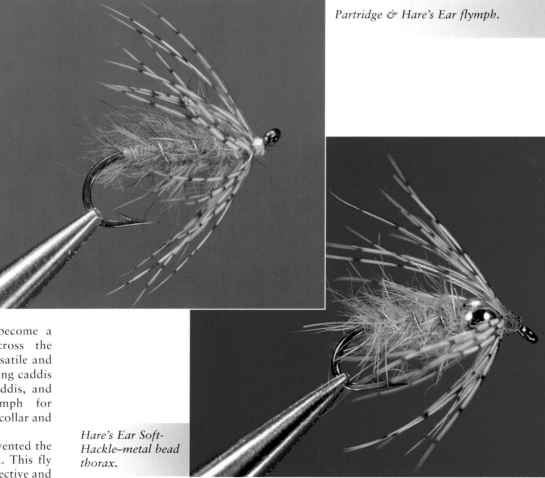

Partridge & Hare's Ear flymph.

Hare's Ear Soft-Hackle–metal bead thorax.

Chapter Two

TRADITIONAL AND
MODERN *Tying Techniques*

If there were one surefire way to become a better fly fisherman it would have to be by tying your own flies. When you tie your own flies, you better observe the natural insects in order to mimic an effective reproduction. Through this observation you will better understand the insects of a trout stream's ecosystem. You are no longer a casual observer, but instead a participant with any pattern you have created. You're also no longer at the mercy of a fly shop's limited selection and frequently incorrect size and color of the stage of the natural that you need to imitate. I see tying flies as the other half of being a fly fisherman, an essential other half.

Soft-hackled nymphs and flymphs provide a wonderful stage with which to begin your fly-tying education or expand your current knowledge base. The materials used are basic and for the most part easily obtainable.

Partridge skin

To begin tying these patterns you only need a few items and out of these can come many pattern variations. Then as your material selection expands you will be able to tie any soft-hackled pattern whenever you need to. I will first discuss the materials used to tie these flies and each ones beneficial properties. After looking at the choices of various materials we will learn the techniques used to tie specific patterns.

The majority of feathers used for tying the soft-hackle collar on wet flies come from upland game birds both here in the United States and from overseas, particularly Western Europe and Asia. These feathers include skins or wings from Hungarian partridge, grouse, starling,

coot, snipe, jackdaw, chuckar, quail, woodcock, rail, and hen. With the exception of hen and pen-raised partridge many of these feathers are from wild birds that have to be bagged during hunting season. It can be difficult to find some of the legal bird feathers for sale because of the limited supply due to the way they are harvested. Partridge and hen are easy to obtain but even these can be somewhat difficult if looking for a particular feather characteristic such as honey-dun. It's best to go to a fly shop that specializes in hard-to-find materials or become friends with a hunter, if your're not one yourself.

The soft-hackled fly tyer needs to be aware that the feathers of some birds are prohibited for use unless they were legally

hunted by the tyer themselves. The Migratory Bird Treaty Act of 1918 was passed between the United States, Canada, Mexico, Russia, and Japan to stop the commercial trade of native bird species that had been decimated by the use of their feathers to make clothing and other items. This treaty established new laws for the possession of feathers of the listed birds. Migratory birds fall into two categories: web footed and non-web footed. Web-footed birds that migrate, such as ducks and geese, are available for commercial sale. Non-web footed migratory bird feathers, however, are not available for trade, sale, or possession unless obtained in season by a licensed hunter and only used for his own fly-tying.

Species protected under the Migratory Bird Treaty Act include but are not limited to dove, rail, coot, woodcock, sandhill crane, and snipe. The bill protects 83% of the native bird species in the United States and even more are protected under the Endangered Species Act. The exempt species are starling, feral pigeon, and the house sparrow. In addition, resident state bird populations of gray partridge, sage grouse, quail, and pheasants are not included under the bill. Feathers and flies tied with protected bird feathers cannot be found, traded, or purchased. Another law to be aware of is the Songbird Act that protects birds such as kingfishers and jays in the same way as the Migratory Bird Treaty Act. Anglers need to be aware of these laws as they apply before using feathers from any of the listed birds.

When you get a skin or a set of wings make sure they have been properly cleaned and are free of bugs. The skin should be free of fat and oils but not dry and brittle. Look for skins and wings that have numerous feathers to tie the patterns in the hook sizes you plan on using. Avoid buying bulk-packaged feathers, as they don't have all the sizes and color patterns a good skin has. Visually inspect different skins or wings if possible to find the ones that have the desired color and texture you're after.

PARTRIDGE FEATHERS

If I were limited to one feather for tying wet flies it would have to be one from a Hungarian partridge. A quality skin can last years, even if you only tie only soft-hackle wet flies with it. The feathers on the neck are speckled and range from light to dark gray. The lower back feathers are a speckled brown. Partridge feathers do a remarkably good job of giving the impression of the insect's leg segmentation. My favorite soft-hackle feathers are the mottled brown marginal covert feathers located on the shoulders of the wings. These feathers are mottled light to dark brown and have a very webby quality. The fibers also remain rather consistent in length along the feather's stem for a predicable length to the finished hackle. Furthermore, these wing feathers are abundant in 16 and 18 sizes. Partridge skins have a color range of feathers that most other birds don't have, and skins are also available with dyed feathers that can be substituted on patterns to match the naturals found in your area. Some skins have feathers that can tie flies from a size 6 down to a 20 without special hackling techniques. A good skin is to be prized; it will have clean, soft feathers with all the color shades able to tie down to size18. Partridge have almost every shade feather you need to tie any soft-hackle collar and the fibers have unparalleled action in the water.

GROUSE

The ruffed grouse has feathers that are commonly used for soft-hackled nymphs. The body feathers have a dark brown and tan mottled appearance. They make very good feathers for soft hackles in that they are easy to wrap due to their flexible stems and have soft fibers. The grouse feather creates a nice effect on soft-hackled nymphs and is used in tying the Pheasant Tail Stone Soft Hackle and the Orange Hare Thorax Nymph. Feathers used for soft-hackle collars are the back feathers and the marginal covert feathers on the wings. Starling feathers are black with an iridescent blue-green sheen and tan tips.

HEN

barbs. Solid, dense webbing will also allow the feather to soak up water and help the fly sink and stay under water.

Another consideration is using hen saddle feathers. These come from the back of the hen and are wider than cape feathers providing longer individual fiber lengths. An advantage of saddle feathers is that they usually have a very heavy and solid web denseness that is desirable for a lifelike action in the hackle collar. Keep in mind that hen saddle fibers are also somewhat thicker in diameter than those of cape feathers, making the hackle collar appear thicker.

Another useful benefit of hen is that hen feathers of the appropriate color and web content are reasonable substitutes for the protected migratory bird feathers used in many traditional wet flies. Match the hen feather as closely as possible to the characteristics of the migratory bird feather you want to imitate in your fly.

Useful colors include light, medium, and dark blue dun, black, grizzly, ginger, greenwell, brown furnace, silver and golden badger, and honey dun capes and saddles. A true greenwell feather has a black center and ginger tips. Since honey dun and greenwell can be somewhat difficult to find, a ginger feather can be substituted for honey dun and a furnace feather looks similar enough to be used in place of greenwell.

DUCK

Hen feathers may be the most versatile feathers for tying wingless wet flies because of the wide range of colors, fiber lengths, and web denseness they offer. Genetic hen capes are best for medium and small flies because they have shorter barb lengths allowing you to tie smaller patterns. India hen necks are also a good choice at a reasonable price. Whichever cape you choose make sure the feathers have solid webbing extending out to the tips as far as possible. The webby, soft barbs provide more action or movement in the water than feathers that have stiff

STARLING

Duck feathers are unlike other game birds in that their individual feather barbs are denser and larger. These are extremely webby feathers. The marginal covert feathers on the shoulder of mallard duck wings make very good soft hackle collars in particular for imitating dun colored emerging mayfly wings. These feathers have a light to medium blue dun shade. The small marginal covert feathers on the shoulder are usually small enough to tie down to #18. If you need to tie on a smaller hook use the compensated feather wrap method. Green wing teal are similar to mallard duck but they are a smaller bird. As such teal wings have smaller feathers available. Teal feathers are a dark dun color. These feathers are useful for patterns such as a PMD or BWO Ascension Flymph, patterns where a dun colored feather for imitating the mayfly wing is called for.

Starling is very useful for small flymph and soft-hackled nymphs. The feathers are also used as a substitute for many traditional patterns that use protected migratory bird feathers. All feathers on the skin are useful for soft hackles. The back and wing feathers are often substituted for jackdaw and you can find a substitute for a dotterel feather by using a starling undercovert feather which is dun colored with a buff yellow tip.

QUAIL

Quail are under-utilized bird feathers for wet flies. The Bob White quail in particular have very beautiful light brown soft-hackle feathers. These are nice for hackling small flies. The feathers on the skin are a blend of tan, brown, white and gray and have a distinct mottled appearance. Other quail species and wing feather colors that can be used are California quail, Gambles quail, Scaled quail and Mearns quail which all have distinctively unique feather characteristics.

Feathers of birds that are protected under the MBTA may be imitated for their color and texture or action characteristics by substituting commonly available feathers instead.

COOT

The coot feathers appear as navy blue on the bird. When used as a soft-hackled collar they appear a deep blue dun shade. A substitute feather would be from a white duck wing dyed a deep blue dun or a teal duck marginal covert feather on the wing's shoulder.

JACKDAW

These feathers are an iron gray color. They are a traditional soft-hackle feather used to tie some of the North Country spider patterns. They make useful wet-fly feathers when a dark hackle collar is desired. A

substitute feather is a starling body feather. This is the feather James Leisenring used for the Iron Blue Dun wet-fly.

SNIPE

Snipe feathers have been used traditionally for North Country soft-hackles such as the Snipe and Purple. They make a good feather for tying smaller-sized patterns. The feather colors range from mottled brown and black, mottled brown and

white to solid brown and solid white. Grouse can be substituted if the feathers are small enough.

WOODCOCK

These feathers are a mottled tan and brown. The woodcock feather is one of the softest feathers for soft-hackle collars. They have similar mottling and color as brown Bob White quail feathers, which may be substituted for woodcock.

BODY MATERIALS

Selecting the wet fly's body material is just as important as the hackle. On many of the soft-hackled nymph patterns fur is often the material of choice because of the action it displays in the water. The spiky guard hairs are an effective representation of nymphal gills or legs, and the soft fur feels more lifelike, possibly causing the fish to hold onto the fly longer before realizing it's an artificial which gives the angler more time to feel the strike. Hidy stressed the importance of using fur for tying flymphs stating that natural furs have a more desirable texture and a more natural, subtle color as well as the water resistance that provides the air-bubble hydrofuge. Sparser bodies are achieved with thread, floss, synthetic dubbing, turkey biots, pheasant tail, or peacock.

MUSKRAT

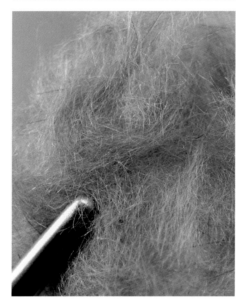

Muskrat makes a nice fur dubbing for body shades of gray. I like to buy muskrat fur on the hide, cut it off and blend it by hand. You don't need to blend this fur in a blender as it is soft and can be done by pulling it apart to blend the fibers into a fine fur dubbing. It also gives me control of how many guard hairs I include for either a spikier or a smoother body. Buy muskrat in the color shade, light to dark, you desire. It can produce a very smooth body if required.

MOLE

Mole fur is a very dark charcoal gray color, almost black. It has few guard hairs and produces a relatively smooth-textured body. I also hand blend this fur from hide patches.

RABBIT

Rabbit fur dubbing is a soft yet buggy dubbing material. Rabbit makes a wonderful dubbing material for nymphs because it absorbs water which helps sink the fly. It comes in many dyed colors and imitates an aquatic insect's body, gills and legs very well. Packaged rabbit dubbing is used to tie such flies as the Scud Soft Hackle, the Emerald Caddis, and the Ascension Flymph. Hareline Dubbin, Inc. produces a fine, soft rabbit dubbing in a wide variety of colors that can be used to imitate many invertebrate bodies from buggy-looking caddis to tapered mayflies.

SQUIRREL

Squirrel fur produces a nice buggy wet-fly body. The fibers are spiky and hold air bubbles under water. You can purchase gray squirrel or red fox squirrel depending on the body shade required.

POSSUM

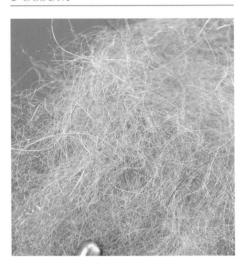

Possum is another good buggy body material. It's softer than, and not as spiky as squirrel. Possum is a good choice for matching an insect's body colors as it comes in a wide variety of dyed shades, often with a mixture of Antron fibers that offer sparkle.

SYNTHETIC DUBBLING

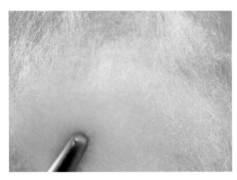

Synthetic dubbing Although natural furs are used on many soft-hackled nymphs and flymphs, synthetic dubbing does make a good material for flymphs that are fished near the surface mainly because you can match the natural's color with synthetic dubbing so well. A fine dry-fly dubbing, such as Wapsi Superfine, is used for some of the soft-hackle emergers and flymphs to imitate the adult dun body color shade. Antron dubbing offers another alternative to the fly's body color. This can be mixed with a fur to add highlights and appeal. Synthetic dubbing doesn't absorb much water and is sometimes factory pre-treated with floatant, as such it's best used for flymphs or surface flies fished high in the water column if they are un-weighted.

ENGLISH HARE'S MASK

Hare's mask fur dubbing is the body material equivalent of what partridge is to the soft-hackle collar. Hare's fur is the most versatile body material. Many tyers are familiar with what is commonly called hare's ear dubbing, but the fur cut from a hare's mask can actually produce dubbing shades ranging from a light orange to very dark brown. Inspect the hare's mask to see that it's a good one. You are looking for one that has all the fur color shades available. Older animals usually produce masks with a wider range of colors. The ears and cheeks should be intact.
Look for a mask that has been dried flat and has clean, bright fur.

1 Fur from the ears is good for dark spiky bodies. The fur from the outer ear is very dark while the inner ear and back of the ears is light brown and white. Ear fur is very stiff and can be mixed with fur from the face for a softer dubbing mixture.

2 Fur located between the eyes is good for tailing as well as body dubbing. You need to clean the under-fur out after you cut the fur off the mask. Doing this will give you more quality fibers and guard hairs in your dubbing. This fur makes a soft medium-dark body dubbing.

3 Crown fur is a reddish-brown shade and is good for a medium body color. The fibers are long and can be used for a lighter-shade tail material.

4 Upper-face fur found below the ears is premium. It is the standard hare's mask dubbing because it's a medium shade containing a balanced combination of light and medium-dark fibers. This fur is used for a standard Hare's Ear Soft Hackle and for thorax dubbing on the Orange Hare Wingless.

5 Cheek fur makes a light reddish-orange dubbing, an example of which can be seen in the Orange Hare Wingless abdomen dubbing.

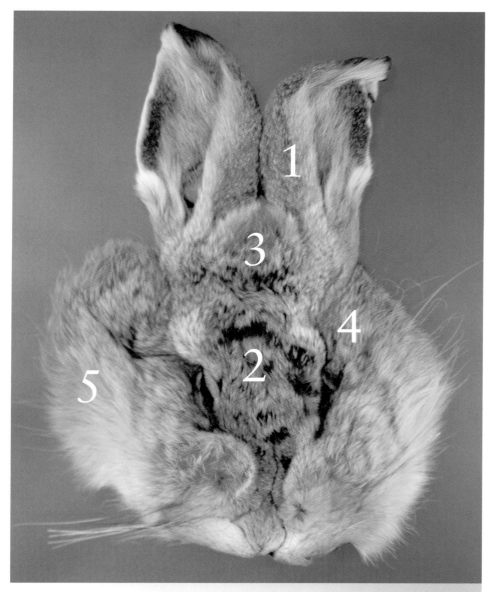

Hare's mask.

PEACOCK

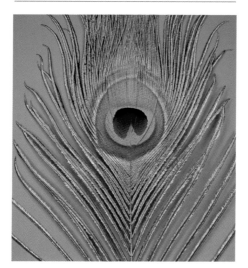

Peacock has a quality that fish find irresistible. To get the best-quality herl buy the peacock eye tail feathers and remove the herl. This herl is superior in quality to packaged herl. Bronze herl can be produced by allowing the peacock herl to be "bleached" by sunlight. Simply place the peacock eye with the herl attached in a sunny location. This could be an indoor window or even on a car dashboard. Turn the herl every day to allow both sides to be exposed to the sunlight. In two weeks or less the herl will have turned from green to bronze. The shade can be adjusted by the length of time that the herl is allowed to be in sunlight. Bronze peacock is used for James Leisenring's Grey Hackle and Red Hackle. Leisenring wrote that peacock herl was the reason why the Red and Gray Hackle were "the most killing general-purpose flies". Green peacock herl is used for tying the Q-Back's and the Red Ass.

Hare's mask dubbing shades.

TURKEY BIOT

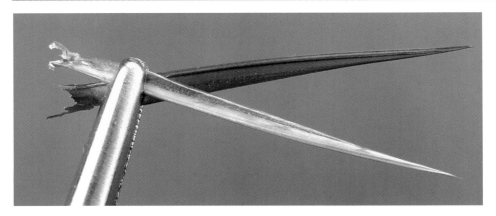

Turkey biots are used to produce sparser, more realistic body characteristics. Patterns that are minimal are often successful in clear, slow waters such as spring creeks where the fish have considerable time to examine a fly. The biot's ridge suggests body segmentation similar to the naturals. They can be tied in for an abdomen with ridged segmentation or one with smooth segmentation depending on the desired effect.

PHEASANT TAIL

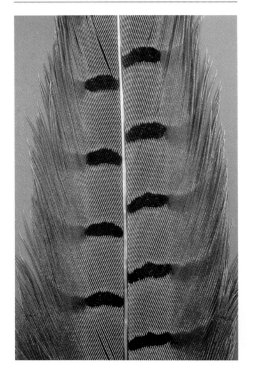

For the ultimate in natural realism I like pheasant-tail fibers. The Pheasant Tail Soft Hackle series are variations of Al Troth's Pheasant Tail Nymph. These patterns provide a very credible imitation of a swimming mayfly nymph. When wet, the pheasant and peacock meld together for a realistic appearance.

When cutting the fur from the skin cut all the way down to the hide. Then separate the fur by pulling it between the thumb and forefingers on one hand into the other. If you want to have more guard hairs in the dubbing mixture make an initial removal of the underfur by holding the fur and guard hair tips in one hand and

pulling the underfur out from underneath them. Many soft furs such as muskrat or mole don't need any more blending than this. However, furs like hare's mask, squirrel, and rabbit need to be mixed in a small coffee bean blender. Use a blender with dull blades to blend the fur and not cut it. Place the fur inside and blend with a pulse of the blades. Just tap the button once this will spin the blades enough to blend the fur. Don't overdue it or you will cut the fur instead of mixing it. Check the fur after a few pulses and see if you like the amount it has been blended. You are looking for a blend that has even fur and guard hair distribution and texture. Remove the blended dubbing and label it in a zip lock bag or dubbing container.

HOOKS & THREADS

Certain hook specifications are necessary for tying these wet flies. The soft-hackled

nymphs perform better with a slightly heavier wire while the flymphs use a dry-fly hook. Pete Hidy used the Mustad 94842 upturned eye hooks for his lightweight mayfly flymphs. Hidy suggests using up-turned eye hooks for flymphs because he felt the flies "somehow look better in the water as they rise toward the surface". I like dry-fly hooks like Tiemco 100's for the emergers on or near the surface, particularly when tying size 20 or smaller flymph patterns. The lightweight 1X fine wire hooks are well designed for flymphs that use sparse material amounts. Soft-hackled nymphs call for a heavier gauge wire to help them sink and to support any lead underbody. I use hooks that have 1X and 2X long shanks for tying nymphs. For these deeper flies my favorite hook is the Mustad 3906B. These hooks are 1X long and are a heavier gauge wire than the dry-fly hooks. The sturdier gauge wire works better for lead wire weight if

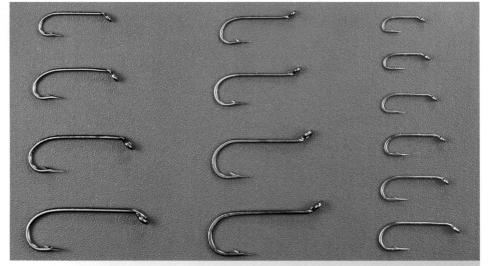

MUSTAD 3906B	MUSTAD 94842	TIEMCO 100
Size 12 - 18	Size 12 - 18	Size 18 - 28

desired. Mustad 3906B hooks are also sufficiently light enough that an un-weighted, heavier-hackled fly will float just by drying it out with false casts. The Mustad 3906B is my first choice for most soft-hackled nymphs and even some flymphs. For soft-hackled nymphs that need a longer hook shank in order to accommodate more materials, I use Mustad 9671 hooks. These are 2X long built from heavy gauge wire and work well for nymphs like the Allen's Drake, the Orient Express, and the bead thorax Red Ass. The artificials tied on 2X long hooks have better proportions because there is plenty of room for the many fly components of these patterns. Other manufacturer's including Daiichi and Dai-Riki make comparable hooks, see the chart below.

UNI-Thread, Gordon Griffith's, Danville Flymaster, Ultra-Thread, Pearsall's Gossamer silk.

SOFT-HACKLED NYMPHS	FLYMPHS
Mustad 3906B	Mustad 94842
Tiemco 3761	Tiemco 100
Dai-Riki 060	Dai-Riki 320
Daiichi 1560(1X long)	Daiichi 1180
Mustad 9671	
Tiemco 5262	
Dai-Riki 730	
Daiichi 1710 (2X long)	

Before you cast make sure your hooks are sharp by holding the fly and lightly running it over a fingernail. If the point digs into the nail a little, it's well sharpened. Wet-fly hooks need to be sharpened before use because when fishing subsurface the hook often is grazing rocks or vegetation that can dull the point and then when a fish strikes the hook won't be able to set deeply or hold. By using a sharp hook your chances of landing the fish will increase tremendously. Buy a hook hone and sharpen the hook before you tie the fly that way you know that all the new flies in your fly box are sharp.

Soft-hackled nymphs are traditionally tied with Pearsall's gossamer silk thread. Silk thread when wet takes on a darker shade than when it's dry and this must be kept in mind when designing the fly to match the natural. It was used by Leisenring and Hidy in conjunction with the spun-dubbing technique to create a translucent body that Leisenring thought to be the most important part of the wet fly's construction. On these flies the silk thread color shows through the dubbing when the fly is wet and appears very much like the natural nymph's semi-transparent body.

When I tie traditional flymphs I still use Pearsall's gossamer silk thread but for the modern patterns I prefer to use nylon or polyester flat thread. For size 10-16 flies my first choice is Danville Flymaster 6/0 waxed thread. Flymaster doesn't build up on the hook quickly which allows for greater latitude in adding materials without bulk and for finishing the thread head neatly. Another good flat thread for larger flies is Wapsi Ultra 70. For smaller flies I choose either UNI-Thread 8/0 or Gordon Griffiths 14/0 thread. I use these for flies from size 18 to 26. Thread choice is very important in helping you create the desired appearance in your flies from building underbody tapers to head finishing. Finally, I use water-based head

cement for finishing the heads and for re-enforcing certain steps for added durability on my wet flies when I'm tying with nylon or polyester thread but I omit using head cement on the silk thread so that the silk will retain its original color at least until wet.

BODY RIBBING

Soft-hackled nymphs usually have ribbing to add an appearance of segmentation similar to the natural insect and sometimes to assist the fly in sinking. The ribbing can be thread, peacock herl, wire, or tinsel. As the thread, wire, and tinsel come in many colors it's easy to choose one to complement the body dubbing.

Flat tinsel, oval tinsel, copper wire, red wire, gold wire.

FLY WEIGHT

Soft-hackled wet flies can be fished deep to imitate nymphs. In order to do this weight is quite often needed. You have to get down to the fish's feeding zone to be successful. In some cases the fly can be tied un-weighted and fished with spit shot on the leader but I find that weighting the fly helps to keep it down in the strike zone better. Under shallow-water conditions a weighted fly is enjoyable to fish without split shot and can be sufficient in achieving a natural bottom drift with help from line-mending techniques. There are many ways to accomplish weighting a wet fly. You can weight the fly with a lead wire underbody or using glass, copper, or tungsten beads tied in as the thorax. A glass bead will sink the fly just under the surface while a brass or a copper bead will sink the fly deeper. For a deep drift in fast water use a tungsten bead thorax in combination with split shot on the leader. Keep in mind the fish's point of view and water conditions when picking the weight to use on your fly. You don't want the fish to be spooked by too-flashy fly. Brass beads over time will tarnish which gives them a duller sheen. This can be advantageous in water conditions where the fish could be suspect of a shiny metal bead. Or you may wish to weight the fly with lead or non-toxic lead for the underbody. Here is a table to illustrate a starting point for the wire and hook size relationship. You can modify the lead wire diameter to suit the pattern weight you desire.

FLY HOOK SIZE	WIRE DIAMETER
18	.010
16	.015
14	.015
12	.020

A bulkier fur body allows you to use a thicker wire underneath but don't overdo the underbody lead diameter. Remember the real aquatic nymphs are sparse creatures and you want to imitate them with your flies. Place the wire wraps on the hook shank so they are underneath the thorax of the pattern, this will allow you to build up a taper from the bend of the hook to the eye and not have a bulky underbody. Something to be aware of is that the hook will ride upside down, with the point up, if you weight the shank with round wire. In order to keep the hook riding with the hook point underneath the shank you can flatten the lead wire with forceps and only weight the front

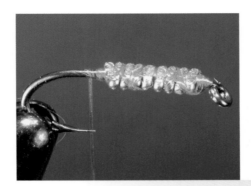

Lead wire flattened to keep the hook riding point down.

half of the hook shank. This is only necessary if the fly is tied with a distinct top and bottom like the Scud Soft Hackle. If you flatten the lead wire do it after securing the wire to the hook shank with the tying thread. This will keep the lead wire from breaking apart when you flatten it particularly when using smaller wire diameters.

BODY DUBBING METHODS

We will now discuss four primary methods of dubbing a wet fly. Each has its own advantages and will impart a different appearance to the body. There is the Leisenring method of spinning a fur body, the Clark spinning block method, the common dubbing loop method, and the direct dubbing method.

The purpose of the traditional Leisenring and Hidy wet-fly body was to allow the tying silk to show through the fur resulting in a lifelike imitation of the natural. James Leisenring used a technique that both rolled and spun the fur to form the dubbing loop. You can get close to the same results using an incorporated spun dubbing loop but Leisenring's dubbing loop not only spins the fur but rolls the fur as well which produces a slightly different effect. His intention was to achieve a dubbing loop that would allow the silk thread, designed to match the color of the intended natural, to show through the fur when wet. When questioned by fellow anglers about his flies and techniques Mr. Leisenring described his fly-fishing philosophy by saying, "You must tie your fly and fish your fly so the trout can enjoy and appreciate it." Leisenring produced his fly bodies with fur or fur-blended materials which he spun between two pieces of silk thread. He felt that the body was what gave his flies their appeal and was the most important part of the fly.

Pete Hidy writes, "If you tie a fly Leisenring style, you will be offering the trout all the characteristics that trout seek in the insects themselves: the fly will appear live and kicking in the currents. The fly will have the iridescence of the living insects, and the subtle coloring possible through the blending of furs and thread. In contrast to a Leisenring creation, a store-bought fly is an artless product tied to a hook with black thread." Fur used for wet-fly dubbed bodies comes from muskrat, mole, arctic fox, gray fox, red fox, rabbit, possum and mohair. The most important fur for a wet-fly body though comes from an English hare's mask. As we have seen these masks contain many colors and textures of fur and a good mask will contain all of them.

LEISENRING SPUN DUBBING LOOP

1 Begin by placing a fifteen-inch-long strand of waxed Pearsall's silk thread on your leg above your knee. The white paper shown here is to allow for a better view of the process.

2 While holding the thread under tension, distribute the fur along the length of thread adding a little more as you progress down the thread to the middle and a little less as you approach the other end. This is a good way to create an evenly tapered body. Keep the thread secure by holding both ends with your thumb and index finger.

3 Fold the un-dubbed thread half over your index finger and center it directly on top of the dubbed fur thread section effectively capturing the fur between the thread.

4 With the thread resting on your leg roll the dubbing loop two or three times in opposite directions with the thumbs of both hands held at right angles to the thread.

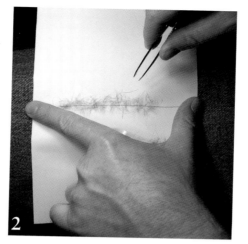

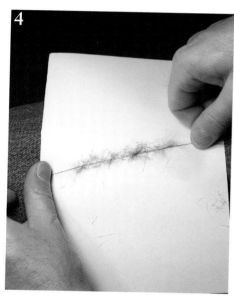

SQUIRREL NATURAL FOX

5 Pick it the loop with both hand and twist it in opposite directions a few more times. The end result is a tightly twisted hollow loop with the fur trapped inside and the thread clearly visible. Leisenring felt the thread needed to be chosen in combination with the fur to imitate the natural nymph's color scheme. Look at a natural mayfly nymph. You will see that the shell is semi-transparent and you can almost see through it. There are at least two colors to the nymphs appearance, that on the outside and that on the inside. This is what Leisenring was trying to imitate with the thread and the dubbing fur.

6 Attach the dubbing loops to a 3.5"x 5.5" notched cardboard card labeled with a description of the fur. Hidy suggests making twelve notches on each side of these cards slightly less than 1/2" apart. Attaching the loops to the card stretches them and allows them to "set" which prevents them from unwinding. Hidy recommends keeping them on the card for several hours or even overnight before using them to tie flies.

CLARK SPINNING BLOCK

Dick Clark, a longtime friend and pupil of James Leisenring, developed a spinning block that simplifies creating the dubbing loop. The Clark spinning block is made from hardwood and while the block is not commercially available in fly shops, it can be built with minimal effort. The advantage of the spinning block is an easier dubbing method because the thread is held under tension by the block leaving the hands free to apply the fur and spin the thread. The dubbing block offers the fly tier more control over the amount of materials and where they are placed on the thread. It's also easier to add more than one type of material to the dubbing loop be it a fur or synthetic when the thread is laid out for you. Pete Hidy used a piece of leather, white on one side and black on the other, placed underneath the fur to allow the tier to better visualize the taper he was creating with the fur. A leather strip or any piece of material that has texture to it can be used. However the wood surface of the block itself is suitable for placing the fur on the thread. In order to build a spinning block buy a 5.5"x 3"x 1" piece of wood. Poplar is a widely available wood that is easy to sand and can be stained if you wish. You will also need fine brass nails and a piece of suede or leather to be used as the block's background if you want.

CLARK SPINNING BLOCK

Clark spinning block.

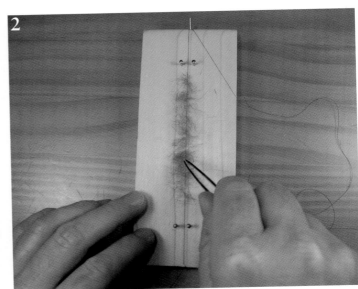

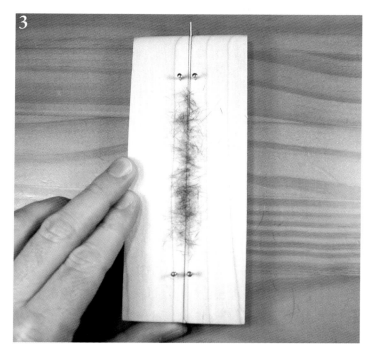

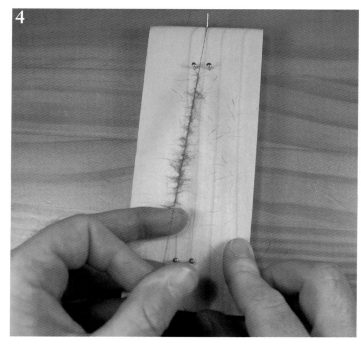

HERE'S MASK NO. 4

After the wood is cut to size, rough out the beveled top edge with a wood plane. Then sand the bevel until it's smooth and even. Next drive a brass nail into the beveled end and cut the nail's head off with linesman pliers. Sand the remaining nail to make it smooth. Then take four brass nails and drive them into the block about 1" from each end and 1/2" apart. If you want to use the leather background cut the leather out using a template and use a hole punch to cut the holes. The leather background is held in place with the nails on the blocks surface. Finally cut a small notch in the end of the block and another one on the side with a razor blade. The bottom end notch should be directly in line with the brass nail post at the top of the block.

1 Attach the waxed Pearsall's silk thread on the dubbing block. First hook the thread in the notch at the bottom of the block. Then run the thread up the block inside the brass nail posts, around the brass nail post at the top, and then hook the thread into the notch on the side of the block.

2 Apply the fur to the waxed thread to achieve a tapered segment. Tweezers makethe job easier. To make a tapered body apply a little more fur to the center of the thread than to the ends.

3 Unhook the side-notched thread and place it on top of the dubbed thread so that you trap the fur inside the loop. Then secure both threads in the bottom notch.

4 Remove both tag ends together and spin them in one direction only. Spin the loop about four or five time by rolling the thread ends between your thumb and index finger. Keep spinning the thread until a tight dubbing rope has been formed.

5 Remove the dubbed loop from the spinning block and place the loop in a notched card. Label the card with the fur used.

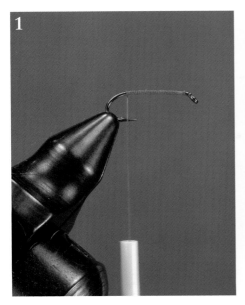

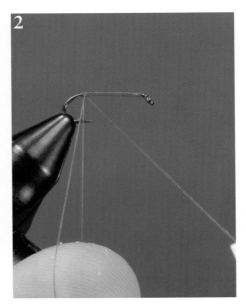

INCORPORATED DUBBING LOOP METHOD

The incorporated dubbing loop method is a popular dubbing technique that allows you to use the thread already on the hook to create a dubbing loop. The fur fibers are trapped inside the loop and spun similar to the other methods above. This method spins the fur in one direction but doesn't roll the loop in opposite directions as does the Leisenring method. The advantages to this method are that the loop is created on the fly itself, not pre-made and then tied in which saves time. Also, there is a relatively low buildup of thread which keeps the fly neat.

1 Build a base of thread on the hook. At the hook bend, or the beginning of the desired dubbing location, pull out about six inches of thread from the bobbin.

2 Place your index finger in the middle of the thread and pull the bobbin around it to create the loop. Make one complete turn of thread around the hood shank to secure the loop. Then make one counterclockwise turn in front of and around the backside of the top of the loop just under the hook shank. Wind the thread over the top of the hook shank and up to the hook eye. Keep the loop open with your index finger.

3 Apply a light coat of wax to the sides of the thread loop.

4 Place the desired fur in the loop spreading it evenly, or with a taper, over all but the bottom of the loop.

5 Remove your index finger while holding the loop together with your thread hand and then attach the hackle pliers to the bottom of the loop. Twist the loop into a dubbing rope.

6 Wind the dubbing around the shank. Preen the fibers back as you wrap it forward so as not to trap any fibers under the loop.

DIRECT DUBBING METHOD

For many wet flies I choose not to use a dubbed loop body, but instead tie them with the direct dubbing technique. I feel that the soft-hackled flies tied with this method are just as effective as the ones tied with the spun loop method because the important aspects of the body are being able to match the correct texture and color of fur to the natural. The number one virtue of any sub-surface fly is for it to imitate a moving, breathing insect. Movement of the body fibers, as well as the soft-hackle fibers, are key to mimicking this life as the fur replicates the gills of the natural and the soft-hackle the moving legs. These moving body parts trigger the trout's feeding instinct. The fish are looking for signs of life in our imitations and not just size and color. With this method I can produce emerger bodies that are fine and sparse or I can dub the body with relatively more bulk and with more fur fiber action. This can be adjusted as I am actually tying the fly and allows me more control over taper and guard hair "bugginess" in the body just by the overlapping wraps I make around the hook. There is minimal thread buildup as each wrap is a single strand of thread as opposed to two strands using a dubbing loop. Neither is there tie-in bulk. When dubbing fur it is important to apply wax to the thread as this method doesn't trap the materials as the spun loop does. The dubbing material holds well when wrapped on the hook if you make close or overlapping wraps to build the tapered body. In order to tie flymphs down to size 26 that require minimal dressings this technique is mandatory. I find there is more control in tapering a body with a direct dub method. With this method you can still achieve the translucent effect of the thread showing through the dubbing but you have to dub the fur sparsely, don't build up the fur on the thread too much. Build a tapered body through overlapping thread wraps as opposed to bulky fur on the thread. Dubbing this way gives you a wider range of choices to the look of the fur body on the soft-hackled fly.

1 Wax the thread at the bend of the hook.

2 Apply dubbing by taking a small amount and using a pinch and twist to evenly attach the fur along the thread.

3 Don't apply the fur too heavy. Allow the thread to show through while at the same time giving the dubbing rope a buggy appearance.

4 The body can be wound in a sparse or bulkier fashion by the amount of turns that overlap as you wind the fur forward.

WET-FLY SOFT-HACKLE PROPORTIONS

A soft-hackled nymph should have certain proportions. These can be altered to achieve different effects. The tail or shuck, if one is used, is usually about 3/4 to 1 full hook shank in length. The density and color of the body dubbing when wet should match the natural. Don't overdress the body. The soft-hackle collar should be sparse so that the body is clear visible when the soft-hackle s are swept back over the fly. Finally, the soft-hackle collar's longest fibers should extend to at least the back of the hook bend and can be as long as a hook shank and a half.

The numbers of turns needed to complete the hackle collar is dependent on the method used to hackle the fly. The hackle should not be over-wrapped. You are trying to simulate legs or emerging wings with the soft-hackle and don't want to make it too thick because the body is an important visual trigger to the fish and must be highly visible through the hackle. Most wet flies require two or at most three turns of hackle. In some cases one turn of gamebird hackle will be sufficient if you desire a sparser look or if the feather has a dense barb count. You need to pay attention to how the collar is shaping up as you wind the hackle and only make enough turns to accomplish the intended effect on the pattern. Jim Leisenring used three grades of stiffness in his hen hackle

feathers. He used a stiff feather for patterns that he fished in fast water. A medium stiff hackle was used for slower water, and a soft-hackle was used for the slowest water situations. This he did because he wanted the water variations to be matched with the variations in the action of the hackle stiffness. He felt this allowed the water to activate the hackle in a more realistic way. You can do this if you want to however I use only soft, webby feathers on all my nymph collars. The action only gets better with faster water

and this action stimulates the fish's feeding instinct. One pattern that I do hackle a little heavier than the others is a Hare's Ear soft-hackle to imitate spent or egg-laying caddis. This pattern needs a thicker hackle collar because the fibers are used to imitate caddis fly wings spread out flat on the water. For winding a standard soft-hackle collar using partridge, hen, grouse, starling and quail. I don't strip the feather. I use both sides of the stem's fibers. When I am tying with duck shoulder or palmering a flymph with a hen feather I like to remove one side of the stems fibers by cutting them very close to the stem with my tying scissors. Another way is to strip the fibers off the stem by peeling them off with your fingers.

On many of these patterns tails aren't necessary. Soft-hackled nymphs, especially the ones fished deeper, are sufficiently equipped with the soft-hackle s extending past the bend of the hook to resemble tail barbs. The trout aren't looking at the tails for a feeding trigger anyway. The closer the fly gets to the surface the more the body construction is scrutinized for realism by the fish. This is why the mayfly flymphs have tails.

The methods I like to use to hackle my wet flies are the Leisenring technique, the standard soft-hackle technique, the stripped fiber wrap, the compensated soft-hackle wrap, and the palmered hackle wrap. All of these produce different results with the soft-hackle fibers.

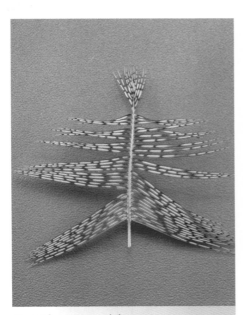

Partridge prepared for tip tie-in.

Partridge prepared for Leisenring style hackling. Notice the two fibers removed from the right side to allow for the hackle to be wound smoothly without trapping them.

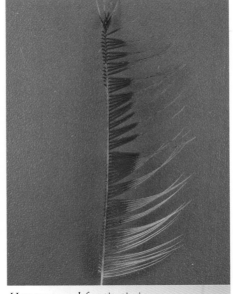

Hen prepared for tip tie-in.

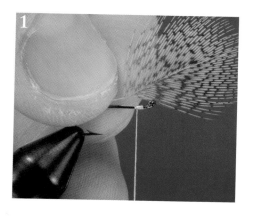

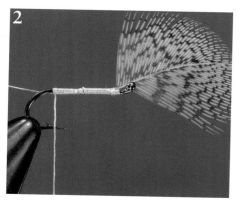

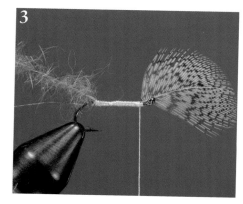

LEISENRING SOFT-HACKLE TECHNIQUE

With this method, the advantages are that since you strip the feather down to the longest barbs you start with the finished hackle length and it's easy to gauge the final results. The result of this method is a sparse hackle with the fibers nicely distributed around the hook and swept back over the fly. I am going to demonstrate the technique by tying a

PARTRIDGE AND HARE'S EAR

Hook: Mustad 94842, size 14
Thread: Gray silk
Ribbing: Gold wire
Body: Hare's mask fur from position
 #4 – top of head
Hackle: Gray partridge feather

1 Prepare a gray partridge neck feather by stripping the downy base and any barbs on both side of the feather, down to the longest barbs you want to include on the fly. Then remove two barbs on the side of the feather that will be wrapped closest to the hook shank. This allows the first wrap around the shank to be smooth. The longest barbs left on the feather should be slightly longer than the hook shank.

2 Start the thread on the hook then-tie in the feather stem about one hook eye behind the hook eye. Wind the thread back to the bend tying in the wire ribbing as you go. If you are using tinsel ribbing wait and

tie it in at the hook bend. Cut the stem if necessary so that the stem doesn't extend past the mid point on the shank. Make sure the thread underbody is smooth.

3 At the bend tie in the pre-dubbed loop that was created using the Leisenring dubbing technique. Hold one of the thread ends with hackle pliers to keep it from un-raveling as you tie in the dubbing loop. Advance the thread to the point where the feather stem emerges from under the thread wraps near the hook eye.

4 Wind the body forward spinning it a little every turn and a half to keep it tight. Take a couple of turns with the thread to tie off the dubbing loop. Then wind the gold wire rib up to the point behind the hackle and tie off with two turns of thread. Trim both the wire rib and the dubbing loop.

5 Take two wraps with the partridge feather placing the second turn behind the first. Then tie-off the hackle with two turns of thread. Trim the remaining feather tip.

6 Pass the thread between the hackle and build up a neat thread head.

7 Whip finish and trim the thread tag end.

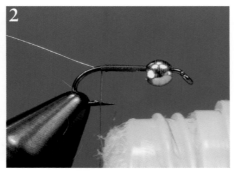

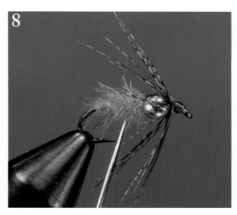

STANDARD SOFT-HACKLE TECHNIQUE

This is my favorite method for size 10-18 soft hackle collars. The advantages to this method are quick feather preparation and ease of hackling since the pliable stem tip is wound around the hook shank. Tying in the feather by the tip permits you to wind the more flexible part of the stem around the hook which is particularly helpful in tying smaller flies. By not stripping the feather barbs you have more fibers of the same length in the hackle wrap. You quite often only need to make one turn of the feather to get a properly hackled collar. I will demonstrate this method by tying an

OLIVE HARE'S EAR: THORAX SOFT HACKLE

Hook: Mustad 3906B, size 14
Thread: Brown 6/0
Ribbing: Gold wire
Abdomen: Olive hare's ear dubbing
Thorax: Gold bead 1/8"
Hackle: Brown partridge from
 wing shoulder

1 Place bead on hook. It may be necessary to de-barb the hook at this point or even bend the hook gape open to get the bead on. Bend the hook back into position with forceps after the bead is on the hook. Then place the hook in the vise.

2 Attach the thread at the location where the bead thorax will be. Wrap the thread back to the bend while securing the gold wire ribbing. Apply wax to the thread.

3 Direct dub or use the incorporated dubbing loop to form the body.

4 Wind the abdomen forward and tie off. Then counter-wrap the gold wire and tie off. Wrapping the wire builds a base to hold the bead in place and also to add extra weight to help the fly sink. Make a whip finish and cement the thread. Trim the thread close. Slide the bead over the thread base. The bead should fit snuggly over the thread wraps.

5 Prepare a partridge marginal covert feather for a tip tie-in. The feather for this pattern comes from the shoulder of the partridge wing.

6 Re-attach the thread to the hook in front of the bead. Tie in the prepared partridge feather with three wraps while holding the feather at a 90° angle to the hook shank. Wrap the feather around the hook once or twice to achieve the desired hackle density.

7 Tie the feather off. Clip the remaining stem and form a neat thread head. Whip finish and apply head cement.

8 Take a bodkin and pick out some of the fur fibers from the body to give the fly a more lifelike appearance.

DISTRIBUTED COLLAR HACKLE

This method is good if you have a feather that is otherwise too large for the hook you are using but still has desirable features. When tying small flymphs (#20 and smaller) this is a necessary method because most soft hackle feathers will be too large. Another advantage to this technique is that since all the fibers are the same length you have better control of the density of the soft hackle collar. This method gives the tyer a wide range of feather choices on smaller patterns. I will demonstrate this method by tying one of my favorite mayfly emerger imitations

PHEASANT TAIL FLYMPH

Hook: Tiemco 100, size 20
Thread: Dark brown 8/0

Ribbing: Ultra-fine copper wire
Tail: Brown & white Z-lon
Abdomen: Four pheasant-tail fibers
Thorax: Two peacock herls
Hackle: Barbs from a brown partridge
 back feather

1 Start thread behind hook eye. Take a partridge feather and cut the stem out. Then holding the fibers aligned measure the length of the hook shank with them.

2 Push the barb butts over the hook eye and evenly distribute them around the hook shank. The tips of the barbs should extend out in front of the hook eye the same length of the hook shank. Make a soft loop wrap around them and then a second wrap to bind them to the shank.

3 Wrap the thread up to just behind the hook eye leaving about two thread wraps of space between the barbs and the

hook eye. Trim the feather stem. Wrap the thread back to the hook bend and attach the shuck, wire rib, and pheasant-tail barbs. Trim the shuck slightly shorter than the hook shank.

4 Advance the thread to the thorax tie-in point. Wrap the pheasant tail barbs up to the thorax and counter-wrap the wire rib then tie-in two peacock herls.

5 Make a couple of turns of herl to form the thorax. Then manipulate the thread in front of the hackle barbs. Push the hackle collar back using a bodkin and the sweeping the fibers back across the fly with your fingers. Hold it in place and make a few turns of thread tight against the barbs.

6 Build a neat head and whip finish or use two half hitches on small flies. Then apply head cement.

COMPENSATED COLLAR HACKLE

Soft-hackle feathers have great action in the water, pulsating with life and energy much like the naturals they imitate. If they have one disadvantage it could be that it is hard to tie small flies with them using standard soft-hackle methods because many of feathers don't come readily in smaller sizes. Some partridge, starling, green teal duck, and hen will tie down to 20 but these smaller feathers are few. However you can use larger feathers by employing alternate hackling techniques. The stripped fiber wrap is one method and the compensated soft-hackle wrap is another one. These allow you to use larger feathers that have the right attributes i.e. color, texture, shade, and fiber count. I will demonstrate this method by tying an Emerald Caddis which simulates a caddis pupe. The feather for this pattern is usually a marginal covert from the wing of a partridge which come in quite small sizes. For this demonstration I will use a larger back feather.

Hook: Mustad 3906B, size 18
Thread: Olive 8/0
Ribbing: Copper wire

Abdomen: Creamy-yellow rabbit fur dubbing
Thorax: Two peacock herls
Hackle: Brown partridge back feather

1 Attach thread to the hook behind the eye. Prepare the soft-hackle feather by stroking the fiber so they stand out 90° to the stem. Then measure along the hook shank to find the tie-in point for the feather by holding the feather tip down and moving the feather from the hook eye to the bend of the hook. Stop when the longest feather barbs are extending out over the hook eye the length you want the soft-hackle collar to be on the finished fly.

2 Tie-in the feather by the tip at the location that will result in the longest fibers extending out over the hook eye the

correct distance. Wind the feather forward around the hook two or three times then tie off. Clip the remaining stem.

3 Push the fibers forward so they are extending out over the hook shank. Wrap the thread forward around the fibers to hold them out over the hook eye. Advance the thread up the shank ending about one hook eye behind the hook eye then wrap the thread back towards the bend forming a smooth thread base.

4 As you wrap the thread back to the hook bend, tie in a piece of copper wire as you go. Then wax and dub the rabbit fur onto the thread.

5 Build a tapered abdomen up to the thorax point and tie in two peacock herls to form the thorax.

6 Sweep the soft-hackle fibers back over the body and manipulate the thread in front of the collar. Build a thread head tight against the collar and overlap a couple of turns if you want the fibers swept back more. Make two half hitches to tie off the head on smaller flies and then head cement.

7 Pick out fibers with a bodkin from the abdomen for a buggier-looking fly.

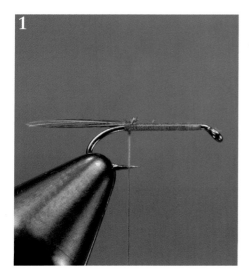 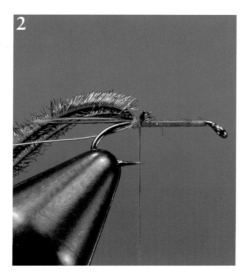 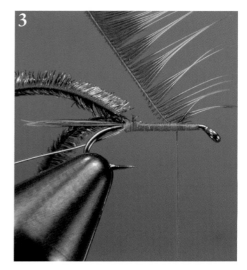

PALMERED HACKLE WRAP

Palmered hackle style wet flies are both beautiful and successful fish-catching flies. The feather is tied in and wrapped differently than the soft-hackle collar wet flies. Hen feathers are good to use as the stem is very flexible and will allow you to make this kind of reverse hackle. The narrow stem also keeps it from being too visible, as you are wrapping the feather on the outside of the body. This technique is demonstrated by tying a

Q-BACK FLYMPH

Hook: Mustad 3906B, size 16
Thread: Red 8/0
Ribbing: Red copper wire
Tail: Four pheasant-tail fibers
Body: Two peacock herls
Hackle: Brown hen neck feather

1 Attach the thread to hook and wrap it back to the bend tying in four pheasant-tail fibers to the shank for the tail.

2 Tie-in the red wire and two to four peacock herls for the body. Advance the thread to just beyond mid-shank.

3 Select a hen neck feather with webby barbs that are slightly longer than the hook shank. Prepare the feather by cutting or stripping the fibers from the side of the feather that is to be wrapped against the hook and tie it in to the top of the shank by the tip. Advance the thread to behind the hook eye.

4 Carefully form a single rope from the peacock herl by twisting it between your thumb and index finger. Wrap the peacock herl up to the hook eye avoiding the feather. Then counter-wrap the wire

and tie off. Trim the ends of the peacock herl and the wire.

5 Wind the hen feather one full turn around the hook shank at the tie in location. Then palmer wrap the feather up the shank to behind the hook eye. As you make each wrap with the feather, stroke the fibers back towards the rear of the fly. It will only take one turn of palmering between the feather tie-in wrap in the middle of the shank, and the collar wrap at the hook eye. Leave space between the palmer wraps. You want the palmering to be obvious.

6 Make two or three turns of hackle behind the hook eye and tie off the feather. Trim the remaining feather stem. Form a neat thread head and whip finish.

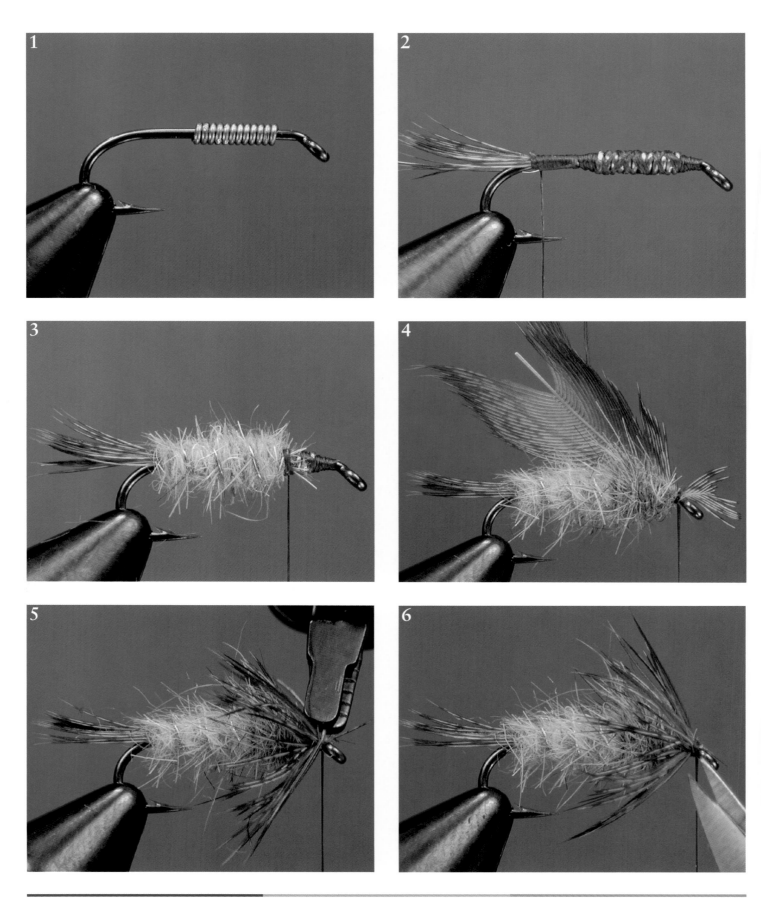

7

For fishing deep or fast currents where the fish are feeding on the bottom you have to get your fly to their level. Split shot alone will not always work to hold the fly at the proper depth so many times it's necessary to tie weight into the fly as well. In shallow-water conditions, a weighted wet-fly can also be fished by itself without split shot. This demonstration will show the procedures to tie a weighted Orange Hare Thorax Nymph. This fly has a shorter hackle collar extending only to the hook point and can be classified as what Leisenring referred to as a short-hackled thorax nymph.

Hook: Mustad 3906B, size 12
Thread: Brown 6/0
Underbody: .015 lead wire
Tail: Grouse
Abdomen: #5 hare's mask mixed with pink Antron
Ribbing: Gold wire
Thorax: #2 hare's mask mixed with pink Antron
Hackle: Grouse

1 Cut a two-inch section of lead wire from the spool. Wind the wire tightly without gaps around the hook to cover the front half of the shank. Trim the excess and slide the wire over the thorax position.

2 Start the thread behind the eye. Cover the shank with thread binding the wire to the hook. Create a smooth thread taper on both sides of the weight. Wrap the thread back to the bend. Tie in the grouse fibers to build a tail. Then tie in the gold wire for the ribbing.

3 Wax the thread and dub an abdomen of #5 hare's mask fur mixed with about 15% pink antron dubbing. Then counter-wrap and trim the gold wire.

4 Dub the thorax using #2 hare's mask mixed with 10% pink Antron dubbing and tie in a grouse back feather by the tip. Size the feather so that the hackle collar extends to the hook point.

5 Wrap the feather to form the desired hackle collar. Trim the feather stem.

6 Build a thread head, whip finish and apply head cement. The hackle collar may be fine-tuned by trimming any errant fibers with a sharp pair of fine-tipped scissors or by plucking the fibers out with your fingers. Trim them as close as you can to the fly.

7 For a buggier fly pick out some fibers from the abdomen and thorax with a bodkin.

As indicated there are many methods that can be used in tying the soft-hackled nymphs and flymphs. You can strictly tie them using a traditional approach or you can tie them using modern fly-tying techniques. But I suggest that you learn to tie the flies using all of these methods and then see which ones you like the best, or should I say see which ones the trout like the best. Even after you have found the ones you prefer keep experimenting. Be creative. Try combining the best traditional methods with the best modern ones, even one's of your own design. Soft-hackled wet flies have been around for a long time. Their history has seen many variations on strategies used to fish them and on new techniques for their creation at the vise. I hope you will continue that legacy and carry these patterns in your arsenal of flies because they scream to be fished as soon as you take that last wrap of thread.

INTRUDER SOFT-HACKLED NYMPH

Hook: Mustad 9671, size 8-18
Thread: Rusty brown
Underbody: lead wire
Tail: Brown Partridge
Abdomen: Peacock herl
Ribbing: Gold wire
Under Thorax: Superfine olive dubbing
Head: Peacock herl
Hackle: Brown Partridge

REALIST PUPA RECIPE CHART

SPECIES	SIZE	THREAD	ABDOMEN	THORAX	WINGLETS	HACKLE
Attractor	10-20	black	brown	natural squirrel	brown	brown partridge
Hydropsyche	10-14	brown	tan	dark brown	brown	grouse
Dicosmoecus	6-8	tan	orange	orange squirrel	ginger	grouse
Agraylea	20-24	black	gray	dark gray	black	starling
Brachycentrus	12-20	black	green	black	brown	grouse

SOFT-HACKLED NYMPH & FLYMPH PATTERNS

ALLEN'S DRAKE

Hook: Mustad 9671, size 8-12
Thread: Brown
Underbody: .020 flattened lead wire, brown dubbing
Tail: Brown ostrich herl
Body: Brown ostrich herl
Ribbing: Copper wire
Bead: Gold metal (optional)
Hackle: Woodcock or Bob White quail

B&B

Hook: Mustad 3906B, size 14-18
Thread: Dark brown
Abdomen: Mahogany turkey biot over thread underbody
Thorax: Gold metal bead
Hackle: Bobwhite quail

ASCENSION FLYMPH-PMD

Hook: Tiemco 100, size 16-20
Underbody: Copper wire to add weight to fly
Thread: Light yellow
Tail: Light dun hackle barbs
Body: Rabbit Hareline Dubbin yellow PMD color
Underwing: Two crystal flash strands
Hackle: Mallard or teal duck shoulder feather
Head: Rabbit Hareline Dubbin yellow PMD color

B&P

Hook: Mustad 3906B, size 14-18
Thread: Olive
Abdomen: Olive turkey biot
Thorax: Peacock herl
Hackle: Bobwhite quail

BIRD'S NEST

Hook: Mustad 3906B, size 10-16
Thread: Tan
Underbody: Lead wire (optional)
Tail: Woodduck mallard flank
Abdomen: Tan opossum
Ribbing: Copper wire
Hackle: Woodduck mallard flank distribution wrap
Thorax: Tan opossum

Blue Dun

Hook: Mustad 3906B, size 12-16
Thread: Primrose yellow silk
Tail: Blue dun hen barbs
Body: Muskrat fur spun on primrose silk
Ribbing: Olive-yellow tying silk
Hackle: Blue dun hen neck feather

BLACK BIBIO

Hook: Mustad 3906B, size 10-16
Thread: Black
Underbody: Lead wire (optional)
Ribbing: Narrow oval silver mylar tinsel
Body: Black rabbit fur separated by red rabbit fur
Hackle: Coot substitute

BRASSIE FLYMPH

Hook: Tiemco 100, size 16-26
Thread: Black
Abdomen: Copper, green or red wire
Thorax: Peacock herl
Hackle: Starling

Brown Hackle

Hook: Mustad 3906B, size 12-16
Thread: Crimson silk
Body: Bronze peacock herl
Ribbing: Narrow flat gold mylar tinsel
Hackle: Brown furnace hen neck hackle

Bukcheon Royal Spider

Hook: Mustad 3906B, size 14-18
Thread: Rusty brown
Tail: Gray partridge fibers (optional)
Ribbing: Red thread
Body: Peacock herl
Rear Hackle: Medium dun cdc
Front Hackle: Gray partridge

BUKCHEON SPIDER

Hook: Mustad 3906B, size 14-18
Thread: Rusty brown
Tail: Gray partridge fibers (optional)
Ribbing: Gold wire
Body: Hare's Ear Plus light dun, yellow, or caddis green
Rear Hackle: Medium dun CDC
Front Hackle: Gray partridge

CRACKLEBACK *(courtesy Ed Story)*

Hook: Dai-Riki 300, size 10-16
Thread: Black or olive
Tail: Furnace rooster saddle
Body: Pale yellow dubbing or turkey rounds
Wingcase: Two peacock herls
Hackle: Furnace rooster saddle

CRIMSON FLYMPH

Hook: Mustad 3906B, size 12-16
Thread: Crimson silk
Tail: Brown hackle fibers
Body: Natural squirrel fur
Hackle: Brown hen feather palmered

ELECTRIC EMERGER

Hook: Mustad 3906B, Tiemco 100, size 14-24
Thread: Olive
Tail: Olive pheasant-tail fibers
Ribbing: Green wire
Abdomen: Olive pheasant-tail fibers
Thorax: Peacock herl
Hackle: Olive mallard flank fibers

DOCTOR LYTE PALMER

Hook: Mustad 3906B, size 12-16
Thread: Orange silk
Rib: Peacock herl
Rib: Narrow gold tinsel in front of peacock herl
Body: Dingy-orange dubbing
Rib hackle: Honey dun slightly smaller than hackle collar
Hackle: Honey dun hen

EMERALD CADDIS

Hook: Mustad 3906B, size 12-18
Thread: Olive
Underbody: Lead wire (optional)
Abdomen: Creamy-yellow rabbit fur
Ribbing: Copper wire
Thorax: Peacock herl
Hackle: Brown partridge from wing

GREY HACKLE

Hook: Mustad 3906B, size 12-16
Thread: Primrose yellow silk
Body: Bronze peacock herl
Ribbing: Narrow flat gold mylar tinsel
Hackle: Yellow or white creamy furnace

HARE'S EAR SHN

Hook: Mustad 3906B, Tiemco 100, size 10-24
Thread: Dark brown
Underbody: Lead wire (optional)
Body: Hare's mask fur #4
Ribbing: Gold wire
Hackle: Brown partridge from wing

HARE'S EAR FLYMPH

Hook: Mustad 3906B, size 12-18
Thread: Crimson silk
Tail: Brown hen hackle fibers
Ribbing: Narrow gold wire
Body: Hare's mask fur #4
Hackle: Brown furnace hen

HARE'S EAR SHN -DARK

Hook: Mustad 3906B, Tiemco 100, size 12-24
Thread: Dark brown
Underbody: Lead wire (optional)
Body: Hare's ear fur #1
Ribbing: Gold wire
Hackle: Brown partridge from wing

HARE'S EAR SHN, GLASS BEAD THORAX

Hook: Mustad 3906B, size 12-18
Thread: Brown
Abdomen: Hare's mask fur #3
Thorax: Brown glass bead
Ribbing: Gold wire
Hackle: Brown or gray partridge from wing

HIGHLAND CADDIS

Hook: Mustad 3906B, Tiemco 3761, size12-18
Thread: Tan
Egg Sack: Caddis Green Rabbit Dubbing
Body: Tan Rabbit Dubbing
Hackle: Bobwhite quail belly feather

HARE'S EAR SHN, METAL BEAD THORAX

Hook: Mustad 3906B, size 10-18
Thread: Brown
Abdomen: Hare's mask fur #3
Thorax: Gold metal bead
Ribbing: Gold wire
Hackle: Brown or gray partridge

HONEY DUN

Hook: Mustad 94842, size 12-16
Thread: Ash silk
Tail: Honey dun hackle fibers
Body: Hare's mask fur #3
Ribbing: Gold wire
Hackle: Honey dun hen neck

IRON BLUE DUN

Hook: Mustad 3906B, size 12-18
Thread: Crimson silk
Body: Mole fur
Hackle: Starling or jackdaw wing shoulder feather

LITTLE OLIVE FLYMPH

Hook: Mustad 3906B, size 16-18
Thread: Ash silk
Tail: Blue dun hen hackle fibers
Ribbing: Olive-yellow silk thread
Body: Olive Superfine or beaver dubbing to match natural
Hackle: Blue dun hen neck

DIVING BAETIS SPINNER

Hook: Tiemco 100, size 16-22
Thread: Olive dun or dark brown
Tails: Dun Micro Fibetts
Egg sac: Olive-yellow or rusty brown dubbing
Abdomen: Olive or rusty brown turkey biot match the naturals color
Thorax: Pearl bead
Wing: Z-wing or gray raffia cut to shape
Hackle: Starling

McGee's SCS *(Spring Creek Special)*

Hook: Mustad 3906B, size 16-18, TMC 100, size 20-24
Thread: Dark brown
Tail: Brown partridge back feather
Body: Pheasant tail barbs
Ribbing: Peacock herl and gold wire
Hackle: Brown partridge back feather extending to bend of hook

MEDIUM OLIVE NYMPH (*G.E.M. Skues*)

Hook: Mustad 3906B, size14
Thread: Olive
Tail: Greenwell hackle fibers
Ribbing: Oval gold tinsel
Abdomen: Olive goose fibers
Thorax: Olive dubbing
Hackle: Dun hen hackle

ORANGE HARE WINGLESS

Hook: Mustad 3906B, size 8-16
Thread: Dark brown
Tail: Grouse
Abdomen: Hare's mask fur #5 mixed with pink Antron
Ribbing: Gold wire
Hackle: Honey dun or brown hen palmered
Thorax: Hare's mask fur #4 mixed with pink Antron

NOEL SOFT HACKLE

Hook: Mustad 3906B, size 10-16
Thread: Black
Underbody: Lead wire (optional)
Body: Golden yellow floss
Ribbing: Peacock herl and copper wire
Hackle: Brown partridge from back
Head: Peacock herl

ORANGE HARE THORAX NYMPH

Hook: Mustad 3906B, size 12-16
Thread: Dark brown
Underbody: Lead wire (optional)
Tail: Grouse
Abdomen: Hare's mask fur #5 mixed with pink Antron
Ribbing: Gold wire
Thorax: Hare's mask fur #4 mixed with pink Antron
Hackle: Grouse

ORIENT EXPRESS

Hook: Mustad 9671, size 10-18
Thread: Brown
Tail: Pheasant-tail fibers
Ribbing: Amber wire
Rear Abdomen: Pheasant tail
Middle Abdomen: Natural squirrel
Thorax: Gold tungsten bead
Hackle: Bob White quail

PARTRIDGE & CHARTREUSE

Hook: Mustad 3906B, size 14-18
Thread: Chartreuse
Abdomen: Chartreuse floss twisted into tight strand
Thorax: Gold or tungsten bead
Hackle: Gray partridge from neck

PALE WATERY DUN WINGLESS

Hook: Mustad 3906B, size 12-16
Thread: Primrose yellow silk
Tail: Honey dun hackle fibers
Body: Amber rabbit fur
Hackle: Honey dun hen

PARTRIDGE AND HARE'S EAR

Hook: Mustad 94842, size 14-16
Thread: Ash silk
Body: Hare's mask fur #3
Ribbing: Gold wire
Hook: Gray partridge slightly longer than hook

PHEASANT TAIL FLYMPH

Hook: Mustad 3906B, Tiemco 100, size 10-26
Thread: Dark brown
Shuck: Brown and white Z-Lon mixed together
Abdomen: Pheasant-tail barbs
Ribbing: Copper wire
Thorax: Peacock herl
Hackle: Brown partridge back feather

PHEASANT TAIL SHN, GLASS BEAD THORAX

Hook: Mustad 3906B, size 12-20
Thread: Dark brown
Abdomen: Pheasant-tail barbs
Ribbing: Copper wire
Bead: Peacock glass bead
Hackle: Brown partridge back feather

PHEASANT TAIL SHN

Hook: Mustad 3906B, Tiemco 100, size 10-26
Thread: Brown
Ribbing: Fine copper wire
Abdomen: Pheasant-tail barbs
Thorax: Peacock herl
Hackle: Brown partridge back feather

PHEASANT TAIL SHN, METAL BEAD THORAX

Hook: Mustad 3906B, size 10-18
Thread: Brown
Abdomen: Pheasant-tail barbs
Ribbing: Copper wire
Bead: Copper metal bead
Hackle: Brown partridge back feather

PRINCE NYMPH

Hook: Mustad 3906B, size 10-18
Thread: Black
Underbody: Lead wire (optional)
Tail: Brown goose biots
Ribbing: Gold oval tinsel or wire
Body: Peacock herl
Wing: White goose biots
Hackle: Partridge or grouse

Q-BACK

Hook: Tiemco, size 100 12-20
Thread: Red
Body: Peacock herl
Hackle: Barred ginger rooster saddle

PT STONE SHN

Hook: Mustad 9672, size 8-10 bend front of hook
Thread: Dark brown
Underbody: Lead wire flattened horizontally behind copper bead
Tail: Grouse feather fibers divided
Ribbing: Copper wire medium
Abdomen: Squirrel fur rusty brown
Thorax: Copper bead 5/32"
Hackle: Grouse back feather
Head: Squirrel fur rusty brown

Q-BACK FLYMPH

Hook: Mustad 3906B, size 12-16
Thread: Red
Body: Peacock herl
Ribbing: Red wire small
Hackle: Brown hen palmered
Tail: Pheasant-tail fibers

REALIST PUPA

Hook: Mustad 3906B, size 12-20 bend rear 2/3 of hook shank down slightly
Thread: Black
Underbody: Lead strip lashed to underside of shank, fine olive dubbing to form taper
Abdomen: Green turkey biot
Ribbing: Black thread 8/0
Thorax: Squirrel black with white Antron mixed in
Winglets: Brown Swiss straw
Hackle: Grouse

RED ASS

Hook: Mustad 3906B, Mustad 9671 (for bead thorax version), size 12-18
Thread: Red
Underbody: Lead wire (optional)
Body: Peacock herl and copper wire twisted to form rope
Thorax: Gold bead (optional)
Hackle: Gray partridge

RED ASS *(traditional)*

Hook: Mustad 3906B, size 12-18
Thread: Red
Tail: Golden pheasant tippets with red antron tag
Ribbing: Copper wire
Body: Peacock herl
Hackle: Silver badger hen

RED POSSUM

Hook: Mustad 3906B, size 6-18
Thread: Brown
Underbody: Lead wire (optional)
Body: Possum Plus dubbing amber
Ribbing: Gold wire
Hackle: Brown partridge from wing

SAWYER PHEASANT TAIL NYMPH (author's variation)

Hook: Mustad 3906B, size 16-18
Weight: Copper wire
Tail: Four pheasant-tail barbs
Abdomen: Pheasant tail
Hackle: Starling

SULPHUR WINGLESS

Hook: Mustad 3906B, size12-18
Thread: Primrose yellow silk
Tail: Honey dun hen fibers
Ribbing: Olive yellow thread
Body: Pale yellow Superfine or beaver dubbing
Hackle: Honey dun hen neck

SCUD SOFT HACKLE

Hook: Mustad 3906B, size 10-20
Underbody: Lead wire flattened horizontal
Thread: Iron gray
Body: Gray or olive rabbit fur to match the naturals, picked out, cut smooth on top
Ribbing: Clear monofilament .009 for #14
Hackle: Light gray partridge feather trim fibers on top

TRANSITION FLYMPH

Hook: Tiemco 100, size 16-22
Thread: Pale yellow
Underbody: Copper wire to add weight to fly
Tail: Pheasant-tail fibers
Ribbing: Fine copper wire
Abdomen: Pheasant tail fibers
Thorax: PMD Superfine, rabbit or beaver dubbing to match natural
Hackle: Brown partridge shoulder wing feather extending to slightly beyond hook point

YELLOW HARE THORAX NYMPH, BEAD HEAD

Hook: Mustad 9671, size 12-18
Thread: Rusty brown
Underbody: Lead wire (optional)
Tail: Grouse
Abdomen: Yellow hare's mask
Ribbing: Copper wire
Thorax: Yellow hare's mask
Hackle: Grouse
Bead: Tungsten or gold metal

TUP'S NYMPH

Hook: Mustad 3906B, size 12-14
Thread: Primrose yellow silk
Tail: Light blue dun hackle fibers
Body: Primrose yellow buttonhole twist thread
Thorax: Yellow and claret seal substitute mixed
Hackle: Light blue dun

ELECTRIC FIRE FLYMPH

Hook: Mustad 3906B, size 12-18
Thread: Rusty Brown
Shuck: Red antron
Abdomen: Medium copper wire and fine green wire
Underwing: Gray antron or Z-Lon
Overwing: Two Krystal Flash strands
Thorax: Gold bead
Hackle: Bob white quail or woodcock

MIDGE SOFT HACKLE

Hook: Tiemco 100, size 18-28
Body: 8/0 thread in black, gray, or brown to match the natural
Legs: Gray partridge

Chapter Three

EQUIPMENT

The long tradition of soft-hackled wet flies has also had a long tradition of fishing equipment to complement them. We now live in a time where we have more fly rods, reels, line tapers, and leader choices than at any other period in angling history. A modern angler can choose the best of the old, the best of the new, or a combination of both. Anglers in Hidy and Leisenring's time were primarily using bamboo fly rods to fish the wet flies. These rods worked well for the methods used for wet-fly fishing, and they still work well now. Traditional wet-fly fishing lends itself to the slower action of bamboo. A bamboo fly rod has many advantages when it comes to fishing wet flies. First of all it needs to be cast with a slower casting stroke than graphite. Usually this translates into the line loop being more open. This helps the fly sink faster by keeping the fly saturated with water and not drying it out as faster line speeds can do. The fly will sink quicker as it re-enters the water this way. A bamboo rod also helps protect light tippets by absorbing the shock from the striking fish. The rod gives more as a result of the strike than a faster material like graphite. This is especially important when you are fishing the fly downstream and the fish has its own weight plus the current putting stress on the monofilament material, the fly connection, and tippet to leader knots. To carry this idea a little further a bamboo rod will actually help in keeping the hook in a fish's mouth because as the hook is set a faster rod will quite often not give and the hook simply pulls out of the fish's mouth. Bamboo rods flex easier and give with the hook instead of against it. Graphite being a relatively stiff material will sometimes pull the hook out while you are trying to get a good set. The use of a slip strike helps set the hook better so I use it whether I am fishing graphite or bamboo. Finally bamboo fly rods are just plain fun to fish. They practically force

you to slow down your casting stroke if you are casting too fast. A quality bamboo fly rod is more than the sum of its parts, it is an extension of the makers personality and quite often becomes part of the anglers as well. A day fishing a bamboo rod seems to imprint itself in your memory allowing you to recall it at will. Maybe it's because bamboo forces you to take a breathe, look at your surroundings, and appreciate the fact you are on trout stream surrounded by beauty fishing a bamboo rod.

With this said it's important to talk about the benefits of graphite fly rods and rod length. Wet-fly nymph fishing is best done with a longer rod from 8' to 9' in length. Also remember that flymph fishing is emerger fishing and is very similar to dry-fly fishing. These longer rods allow you to reach over currents so as to prevent drag. A 9' rod has unmatched mending abilities both when the line is in the air and on the water. Finally a long rod keeps that much more line off the water to begin with which helps prevent the fly line from getting pulled around by the currents causing the fly to drag. Frank Sawyer recognized the advantages of longer rods and used a 8 1/2 to 9' rod for his remarkable nymphing methods. Regarding rod length Sawyer wrote, "To be able to control and move a nymph properly you must have sufficient leverage, and so it is a disadvantage to use a short rod. The trouble with a short rod is that before you have been able to lift the tip high enough to impart, say, a 2-foot drag, there is no leverage left to use for tightening should a fish take. In fact, the rod passes that comfortable position in the hand when just a flick of the tip will set the hook."

With rod length under consideration I find graphite rods to be a better choice in large part due to their lightweight construction. A graphite fly rod of 8'-9' is presently the ultimate fly fishing tool. Graphite rods will not tire your arm as fast

as bamboo as graphites usually weighs ounces less than bamboo in the same length and line weight. Over the course of a full day on the water this can be a significant advantage. Graphite rods being lighter also seem to aid you in line mending. It's easier to throw upstream or downstream mends with a lighter rod and you will be more apt to make the mends because they will not be as laborious. Due to graphite's inherent stiffness it's easier to pick up and mend the line on the water with just a flick of the rod tip. The weight issue is also a factor when you are doing a lot of high-stick wet-fly nymphing. A lighter rod is just more comfortable to hold at a high level parallel to the water. Joe Humphreys prefers graphite rods because as he says, "the thing about bamboo is you get deeper shock waves in your line off the rod tip on the backcast, so you have to drift the rod a little further forward before you make the forward stroke. Graphite's much more forgiving; the shock wave on your backcast from graphite are very shallow. You can apply a shorter stroke on the forward cast to get the job done with graphite".

Regarding the casting of weighted leaders or large weighted flies graphite rods handle the weight better as well. I fish graphite rods most of the time, but when I just want to have a relaxing day on the water, slow things down, and maybe be a bit nostalgic I will fish my bamboo rods.

Trout fly reels don't need to be complex to get the job done. I favor the single-action-click-and pawl reels. These reels are light and uncomplicated. They need very little maintenance and are dependable. I have never been in a trout stream situation where I have needed more drag than they offer. By using the pawl gears and the drag knob in combination with palming the spool's exposed rim you have infinite control over how fast your line runs. The important thing is to make sure your reel has almost no start-up inertia that could break your tippet. I like my reel to be set at as low a drag setting as possible. Wet flies are often fished across and downstream and when the fish is hooked in these situations the initial run is quite fierce. Your reel is going to want to spin instantly and if it can't the tippet or fly is going to separate. If you are going to use a reel that has a disc drag just make sure the drag is set very light. The excitement of fishing these wet flies is that the trout will often strike the fly hard and your reel should be ready for the task without you having to adjust it while trying to play the fish, if you even get the opportunity to before the tippet breaks. Also when fishing downstream a hooked fish can the use fast currents to its advantage and any runs it might make will need to be gingerly negotiated by you and your equipment. A smooth, light drag setting will take a great deal of pressure off your tippet.

The next important consideration of your equipment is the fly line. I prefer a floating line and preferably one that is sufficiently visible on the water. This visibility of the line aids in tracking the flies float and detecting sub-surface strikes. It also assists you in seeing the current's play on the line and alerting you into make necessary mends to counteract this drag. The color of the fly line should be chosen based on this visibility issue. As far as line color I prefer a subtle yet visible line such as buckskin or tan. These are highly visible but don't stand out in nature's color scheme. The color of the fly line however is secondary to the taper. Floating line tapers usually comes down to deciding between weight-forward lines and double-taper lines. I prefer double-tapered because I like how I can mend the line in the air and on the water with this line. If I have forty feet of line out and want to make a reach mend in the air I'm not back behind the front taper trying to do it with the running line as would happen if I was using a weight-forward line. The same idea applies when the line is on the water. I don't want to have to deal with the line hinging when I get past the belly portion. With a double-taper line you are always turning over the same diameter or a smaller diameter line. Furthermore a double-taper line has a slightly longer transition length between the belly and the tip. This will assist in you in fishing the soft-hackled nymph because it means that the fly line will sink a little easier when pulled under the surface by weight that's

attached to the leader or built into the fly. It won't be quite as susceptible to buoying up to the surface as a weight-forward line thus keeping your fly down in the strike zone longer. This also slightly reduces the chance of drag because the currents don't have as much line mass to have an effect on. Finally there is the economic consideration. After half of the line shows signs of becoming worn it can be turned around and you have a new half. A double-taper line can last years with proper cleaning and care. Always keep your fly lines away from sources of heat and clean and dress them as the manufacturer recommends for maximum performance.

The line-to-leader connection is also a significant element. There must not be too abrupt a change in material stiffness from fly line to leader butt, if there is there will be a hinging of the cast with the leader either standing up and not turning over or turning over too quickly driving the leader down rather than out in front. There needs to be an efficient transfer of energy from the line to the leader. For this to happen you must match the diameter and stiffness of the fly line to the diameter and stiffness of the leader butt material. The leader butt should be approximately 2/3 the diameter of the fly line. One way to get a rough estimate is to add 16 to your fly line weight. For example if you were trying to figure out the diameter of the leader butt for a 4 weight line you would add 16 plus 4 getting 20. This means you would use a monofilament with a .020 diameter for coming off the fly line. However not only do you need to match the diameter of the leader butt to the fly line, the stiffness of both materials needs to be considered as well. You can test to see how close the stiffness of the line and leader butt are to each other by making a loop with about three inches of material pinched between your thumb and index finger. Then press down on the top of each loop noting the resistance. Test both fly line and potential butt material this way. They shouldn't be too dissimilar.

For the leader butt I like to use Maxima Chameleon. I first tie a butt section to my fly line with a needle nail knot. Then I tie a 1/2" perfection loop in the Maxima 4 3/4" from the end of the fly line. I then attach the leaders with a loop-to-loop connection. This enables me to switch leaders and keep a consistent leader length since no section is cut back except for the tippet which can be added as needed.

Leaders are perhaps the most important part of your equipment set-up. The leader can either help or hinder your casting and fly presentation. It must smoothly transmit the energy from the fly line to the fly in a way that the leader turns over correctly and allows the fly to land accurately. Above all, the leader must allow the fly to drift in a natural way. These are the leader formulas I use for soft-hackled nymphs and wingless wet flymphs.

8' RAY BERGMAN MULTIPLE WET-FLY LEADER
- 16" .015 Monofilament
- 16" .014 Monofilament
- 16" .012 Monofilament
- 16" .010 Monofilament dropper #1 at blood knot
- 16" .009 Monofilament dropper #2 at blood knot
- 16" .008 Monofilament point fly

8' 11" 5X JOE HUMPHREYS NYMPH LEADER
- 15" .017 Maxima Chameleon
- 15" .015 Maxima Chameleon
- 15" .013 Maxima Chameleon
- 12" .010 Soft Monofilament
- 12" .009 Soft Monofilament
- 12" .008 Soft Monofilament
- 26" .006 Soft Monofilament

8' 11" 4X JOE HUMPHREYS DROPPER FLY NYMPH LEADER
- 15" .017 Maxima Chameleon
- 15" .015 Maxima Chameleon
- 15" .013 Maxima Chameleon
- 12" .010 Soft Monofilament
- 12" .009 Soft Monofilament
- 12" .008 Soft Monofilament
- 26" .007 Soft Monofilament tie dropper fly as a 4" extension of the tippet knot

8' 11" 3X JOE HUMPHREYS NYMPH LEADER
- 15" .017 Maxima Chameleon
- 15" .015 Maxima Chameleon
- 15" .013 Maxima Chameleon
- 12" .011 Soft Monofilament
- 12" .010 Soft Monofilament
- 12" .009 Soft Monofilament
- 26" .008 Soft Monofilament

12' 7X GEORGE HARVEY SLACK LEADER
- 10" .017 Maxima Chameleon
- 20" .015 Maxima Chameleon
- 20" .013 Maxima Chameleon
- 20" .011 Maxima Chameleon
- 12" .010 Soft Monofilament
- 12" .007 Soft Monofilament
- 18" .005 Soft Monofilament
- 30" .004 Soft Monofilament

12' 6X George Harvey Slack Leader
- 10" .017 Maxima Chameleon
- 20" .015 Maxima Chameleon

- 20" .013 Maxima Chameleon
- 20" .011 Maxima Chameleon
- 12" .010 Soft Monofilament
- 12" .008 Soft Monofilament
- 18" .006 Soft Monofilament
- 30" .005 Soft Monofilament

12' 5X GEORGE HARVEY SLACK LEADER
- 10" .017 Maxima Chameleon
- 20" .015 Maxima Chameleon
- 20" .013 Maxima Chameleon
- 20" .011 Maxima Chameleon
- 12" .010 Soft Monofilament
- 12" .008 Soft Monofilament
- 18" .007 Soft Monofilament
- 30" .006 Soft Monofilament

In his monumental work *Trout*, Ray Bergman explained about the effectiveness of a 6'-9' multiple wet-fly leader with two droppers and point fly for heavy pocket water. He used this leader with three large #6 bushy wet flies. This method works best in fast, pocket water targeting the areas around rocks and eddies where trout can hold out of the stronger currents. Bergman used many wet-fly techniques including mending the line while swinging his flies to get a more natural and extended drift. He also used the fly reel as a presentation method to retrieve a fly or team of flies when they had completed their swing and where hanging in the current below him, often getting vicious strikes while reeling in the flies. Furthermore, he was a big proponent of the hand twist retrieve while fishing wet flies.

I fish the 8' 11" nymph leaders when I need to get deep and I'm not as concerned with surface-feeding fish. The shorter leader is easier to control and to feel strikes. You will find that these nymph leaders are versatile. They are designed to be fished with split shot as needed and weighted or un-weighted soft-hackled nymph or nymphs for a dropper fly. The split shot goes from 8"-14" above the point fly depending on how near the bottom of the stream you want the fly to drift. BB split added for a bottom drift is adequate for most situations. If you need a deeper drift use two or three split shot. The shot in combination with a weighted nymph and tuck cast should get you as deep as you will need to get with a floating fly line. If the stream section you are fishing is shallow, only a foot or so deep, you might not need any split shot only a

medium-weight wet-fly and mending techniques to get to the bottom. Another setup to use in shallow-water situations is a weighted soft-hackled nymph as a dropper fly and a lightweight flymph as the point fly. The heavier dropper fly will drift along the bottom, while the point fly will be higher up in the water column determined by the tippet length. This enables you to fish the stream bottom and just under the surface at the same time. In multiple fly nymph leaders an effective combination is a larger heavier #1 dropper nymph such as a Prince Nymph followed by a smaller dropper #2 like a bead thorax Electric Fire Flymph and a un-weighted point fly like a Pheasant Tail Soft Hackle. The Prince Nymph dropper will tumble along the bottom, the Electric Fire Flymph will at times be on the bottom and at times ride off the stream bottom, and the un-weighted Pheasant Tail Soft Hackle will be much higher off the bottom even near the surface in shallow water. This system will allow you to effectively fish three levels of the water column and show fish three different styles of nymphs at once. The weighted flies will balance the system and provide a natural drift making split shot un-necessary. Experiment with dropper leader systems so that you are covering different levels and nymphal life stages all at one time by using a combination of heavy, medium, an un-weighted flies on your leader. For fishing the flymph by itself to sophisticated trout a longer leader is necessary. In this case the 12' Harvey leader is used for fishing the emerging flymph patterns, such as the Transition Flymph. This leader will help you achieve a drag-free drift by allowing the leader to land on the water with S-curves that extend through the length of the leader from the end of the fly line to the fly. This is usually achieved in combination with a casting technique such as the slack line cast originated by George Harvey. Line mending-techniques are also used to achieve a natural swing and rise from the flymph. You can lengthen the tippet on any of these leaders to get either a deeper drift or an extended drift through a specific zone under water.. Quite often I will extend the tippet on the 12' leader out to four feet which gives the leader more S-curves up to the fly in a slack-line cast or in the case of one of the induced swing casts, allows the fly to have a more subtle play in the currents. I will discuss more

about how to fish soft-hackled nymphs using these leaders in the Presentation Strategies chapter.

The use of strike indicators is an individual preference. I personally don't use floating indicators for the following reasons: First of all, in heavily fished shallow, clear streams, fish that get caught and released regularly may learn to associate bright indicators with being caught and thus stop feeding at the sight of them. Secondly, large indicators such as yarn indicators can cause the nymph to drag as the indicator is blown across the water surface on windy days. Thirdly the wind resistance of indicators interferes with casting, particularly when there is also split shot on the leader. Fourth, an indicator regulates the nymph's drift at a fixed level-sometimes too high, lifting if off the stream bottom, and sometimes too low, allowing excess slack in the leader when a nymph comes in contact with the stream bottom. In the later case the slack in the leader actually makes strike detection subtler because there isn't a direct connection with the fly. Fifth, they restrict the tuck cast by creating a hinge point that causes the leader not to tuck like it should. Finally, a strike indicator drifts at the same velocity as the surface currents, which are often faster than the sub-surface stream-bottom currents. This pulls the nymph along at a faster rate than the naturals are drifting.

Without the floating indicator the angler is allowed to control the depth of the nymph's drift with rod-tip angle adjustments relating to water-depth changes. Fishing without an indicator also forces the angler to develop his sense to "see into the water"; that is being able to visualize from the end of the fly line to the location of the fly under water and know exactly where and how fast the nymph is drifting. Acquiring this skill also improves other aspects of angling, such as reading the water and locating feeding lies. The Canadian fly-fishing writer Jim McLennan teaches his students to, "Find a reason to set the hook some time during the drift." He says telling his students this, "helps them intensify their concentration and to expect a strike instead of being surprised by a strike." That's exactly right. Sensing a subtle strike when nymphing without a strike indicator requires lots of practice on the stream and concentration throughout the fly's drift. It is important to keep excess slack out of the line while maintaining good line and leader control, yet still allowing the fly to behave naturally. Eventually you will develop the ability to "see into the water" and detect the subtle signals that indicate you should set the hook.

However, there is a way to build a strike indicator into the leader itself that doesn't affect casting or the drift of the nymph. This is called a "hot butt" leader. To build this leader use fluorescent red Amnesia butt leader material in the butt sections of the Humphrey's 8'11" leaders. For instance, use a 15" section of #20 Amnesia which is .019 in place of the 15" section of .018 Maxima Chameleon. If you want even more visibility you can use another 15" section of #15 Amnesia in place of the .016 Maxima. This gives you either 15" or 30" of high-visibility leader that doesn't affect casting, the nymph's drift, or the tuck cast's hinge. With this system you won't be prone to staring at a floating indicator, but will still have a visual aid to track the drift of the fly and signal strikes.

Polarized sunglasses are also essential. They allow you to not only spot fish, but to watch the trout's behavior and in clear water see the strike. When you are fishing sub-surface wets and can watch the fish react as your fly approaches you stand a very good chance of detecting the strike. If your nymph is near the location of a feeding fish and you see a white flash in the vicinity of where the fish's mouth should be, it quite often is the fish opening its mouth and inhaling your fly. In this case use a slip strike or lift the rod tip slightly to set the hook. This kind of sub-surface sight-fishing is the most exciting form of visual fishing for me now. When you can see the trout's behavior under water and the reaction to your presentation it can rival even dry-fly entertainment. I prefer tan lenses in my sunglasses as they take the glare off the water, but still give you good light levels for looking in shaded stream areas. Along with sunglasses, a good wide-brimmed hat will help you see into the water and cut the glare.

Now that you are properly equipped let's go out on the stream and examine how to present the soft-hackled nymphs to the trout.

Chapter Four

PRESENTATION
Strategies

Fly fishermen are always in quest of the ultimate fly for meeting an on-stream situation. But there is much more to it than just finding the perfect fly. An ideal presentation of a fly that isn't an exact match of the natural is going to catch more fish than the exact fly fished poorly. Thus by being able to combine well-executed presentations with lifelike flies you give yourself the opportunity to catch trout consistently on a variety of streams. Fishing these wet flies effectively calls for casting and line-handling techniques that present the fly in a way that looks convincing to the fish. Like the versatility of the soft-hackled wet flies themselves so are their presentation techniques. Remember that the intended result is to activate the soft-hackle collar fibers that make these flies look alive. When deciding on which presentation to use, keep in mind where the natural that you are trying to imitate lives and how that insect moves in the water. This knowledge will assist you in choosing a convincing approach.

CLASSIC WET-FLY SWING

Many of the casts for fishing soft-hackle nymphs have methods based on the classic wet-fly swing. The wet-fly swing cast is accomplished by first making a standard overhead straight line cast up and across stream to allow the fly to sink to the intended level. As the fly passes across stream alongside the angler and then drifts downstream, the line begins to tighten in the current and swing across stream ending in the fly being directly downstream of the angler. The strike can come at any point in the drift so be prepared. Quite often the strike will come when the fly is swinging across stream. This is because as the fly swings it also rises to the surface, a behavior similar to the natural mayfly, caddisfly, or midge pupae.

An on-leader dropper has been used by traditionalist English wet-fly fisherman for years. The fly's held in place by a blood knot and the simplicity helps keep the fly from tangling around the leader or the other flies on a multi fly leader.

The hook-eye dropper is made by attaching a short section of tippet (10"-16") to the hook eye of a fly and tying a point fly onto this tippet section.

The blood knot dropper is a 4"-6" tag end of the heavier of the two mono leader sections. This is a traditional dropper method used by English Clyde-style wet-fly fishermen for their cast or team of wet flies. The short, heavier mono section helps keep the dropper fly from tangling around the leader.

CLASSIC WET-FLY SWING

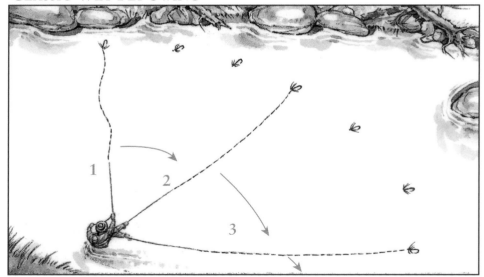

1 Make the cast up and across stream.

2 Follow the fly with rod tip through the drift slowly lowering the rod tip and keeping it pointed towards the end of the fly line as the fly begins to swing. The fly will swing across the current and downstream of the angler.

3 As the fly finishes its swing keep the rod pointed downstream towards the fly.

THE INDUCED TAKE METHOD

Wet-fly fishing allows for considerable input from the angler. The flies are often fished with manipulation from the angler or the current. A fish can be coaxed into striking with a method called the induced take. The induced take is a method that was detailed in writing by Oliver Kite, but invented by Frank Sawyer. Both of these tremendous nymph fishermen often fished their nymph patterns with movement imparted through their presentation techniques. Kite writes, "Successful nymph fishing is primarily dependent on the life-like employment of the artificial by the angler" in his 1963 work *Nymph Fishing In Practice*. Frank Sawyer talked about fly manipulation in *The Master on the Nymph*, "When fish are lying in feeding positions they see many things other than food animals floating by, and all these are disregarded. But should it happen that something like a nymph, floating inertly, suddenly starts to swim in one direction or another, then the eyes of the fish are immediately attracted to it and the thought must be registered that it is a living creature and therefore edible."

This method calls for a short rod twitch or rod-tip lift that increases the speed of the fly usually up towards the surface making the fly appear as if it is fleeing or emerging. The induced take appeals to the fish's predatory instinct to strike either out of spotting a meal or in the case of large flies, striking out of territorialism. Some of the ways to induce a strike are by stripping the fly in front of the fish, lifting the rod as the fly swings, by shaking the rod tip slightly, or by doing nothing but letting the fly swing naturally or hang in the current below the angler. A little fly manipulation goes a long way and slight movements are usually most effective.

LEISENRING LIFT

Although this was not the only presentation method that James Leisenring used it is his most famous as it is the only one he described in the book *The Art of Tying the Wet-Fly* which was mainly a fly-tying book. He had planned on writing another book with Hidy about the presentation methods, but never did. There were other methods he used, however this is the only one we have a description about from Leisenring himself.

Leisenring advocated a kind of induced take. His technique is known today as the Leisenring lift. One difference between the Leisenring lift and Sawyer's induced take is that Leisenring's method involved drifting the fly along the stream bottom until it is just in front of the fish and then the fly comes to life and "becomes deadly" as it looks like it is swimming up to the surface, a movement that trout find irresistible.

THE INDUCED TAKE METHOD

1 The cast is made and the fly enters the water. Lower the rod tip, following the fly through the drift allowing the fly to sink.

2 As the fly nears the fish's holding location, begin to lift the rod tip while still following the fly.

3 The fly rises to the surface and swings across the current at the same time.

LEISENRING LIFT

1 Make the cast across stream about fifteen feet above the fish. Make a short tug with your line hand to straighten the line and leader if necessary to have line and leader control. Allow enough slack in the line to let the fly drop to the stream bottom and drift without being dragged out of the feeding lane.

2 With the rod, follow the fly through the drift with a slack-free line while still allowing the fly to drift on the bottom of the stream.

3 The fly begins to approach the fish. When the fly is about four feet above the fish check the rod by stopping the rod from following the fly's drift. This will cause the fly to begin to swing across the current, rising to the surface and activating the soft-hackle fibers.

4 If you wish to further speed up the fly's rise to the surface raise the rod tip slowly a moment after making the rod check. The action the fly exhibits with these methods will often trigger a fish's predatory instinct to strike.

Whereas Sawyer's induced take is more suited to fishing higher in the water column just under the surface. Leisenring fished the "lift" on Brodhead Creek, a stream that has many flatwater runs of two to four feet that are ideal for this method. The lift is best executed in water conditions that aren't too deep, fast, or with multiple crosscurrents as the line is cast straight and needs to be fished in current that won't belly it before the "check" is made and the fly lifts to the surface. In complicated riffle water, the angler will need to make necessary mends that keep the angler in control of the fly yet also keep the fly drifting in the current seam that the target fish is in. The Leisenring Lift is executed by casting up and across stream beyond the trout's known or suspected position in the water. After the line lands, make a short tug on the line if needed to straighten the leader. Allow the fly to drift on the bottom of the stream without un-necessary slack in the line. When the fly is about four feet above the trout, check the cast by stopping the rod from following the fly through the drift and allowing the fly to swing toward the surface. Lift the rod tip to further speed this ascent. This method results in the fly rising or emerging from the stream bottom toward thesurface like the natural. This is a vulnerable time in the life cycle of the nymph or pupae because the insect is trying to free itself from not only its shell, but the water tension of the surface as well. The check and lift will cause the soft-hackle fibers to pulsate and move creating the impression of life. Leisenring even had a term for this surface ascension and the technique for producing it, calling them "making the fly become deadly."

HIDY SUBSURFACE SWING

This cast was invented by Pete Hidy yet he never fully described it in detail in his writings. Dave Hughes knew Pete Hidy and was able to get a description from him about how he fished his flymphs. This cast is more directly targeted to rising fish than other wet-fly casts. To perform the Hidy subsurface swing, position yourself at about a 30-45-degree angle above the fish. Make a straight-line downstream cast, landing the fly a couple of feet above the rising fish. After the fly lands, immediately tug on the fly line which will pull the flymph under water. Allow the fly to swing across current into the fish's window.

HIDY SUBSURFACE SWING

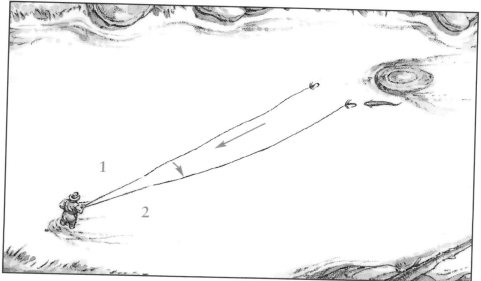

1 Make a straight-line cast and across stream about two feet above the fish.

2 After the fly lands, tug on the fly line to pull the fly under the surface. Allow the current to swing the fly in front of the fish.

THE TUCK CAST

1 Make a standard overhead backcast. Keep the rod in a vertical plane to the water when making the backcast.

2 Begin the forward casting stroke. When the rod reaches 10:30, check the cast by stopping the rod abruptly. In the same instance you check the rod apply a simultaneous motion of squeezing the rod handle by pushing down with your thumb and pulling up on the back of the handle with your pinky and ring finger with assistance of a short forward wrist snap.

Raise your whole arm up a couple of inches, keeping the rod in the same position.

3 Allow the rod to unload the energy into the line, leader, and out to the fly. The nymph will tuck under the line and leader diving into the water first and sinking to the bottom quickly. The rod is now in a high-stick postion that allows the wet fly to be fished with a drag-free bottom roll (see high-stick nymphing), but the cast can now also be used with any of the line drift presentations.

THE TUCK CAST

The tuck cast is a method of casting that allows the fly to reach the stream bottom quickly. It results in helping you achieve a drag-free bottom drift because the line isn't dragging before the fly reaches the fish and causing the fly to be pulled up to the surface and out of the strike zone. The cast is started with a standard overhead backcast. As the fly line begins the forward cast, apply a little extra power to the casting stroke. The rod hand then needs to squeeze the cork grip with the thumb, driving down and into the grip and the pinky and ring fingers pulling up on the back of the grip. The action is performed with a wrist snap and is a little like hammering a nail using your wrist only while squeezing the handle at the same time. As you squeeze, snap the wrist forward, but hold your upper and lower arm still. Don't drop the level of the rod, but instead allow the rod tip to throw the snap into the line. The end of the fly line will make a 90-degree angle down towards the water. The leader will drive straight down and tuck back under the line. The fly will enter the water first and dive to the stream bottom. The rod will then be in a position to fish out the drift. Here you have a cast that shoots the fly to the bottom and also keeps you in contact with it after the cast is made. This enables you to fish your wet flies deep.

The tuck cast is especially useful for high-stick nymphing techniques. High-stick nymphing is usually thought of as being close-in work. However on longer casts using the high-stick technique of raising the rod as the fly drifts back towards the angler, or drifts by the angler when fishing across stream, is important to keep the line from bellying and dragging the fly. This will result in a longer natural drift and keep the fly from rising to the surface. In addition, when fishing fast pocket water close to you, this cast can keep you in direct contact with the fly, allowing you to feel any strike since only the leader, fly and possibly a very little line is on the water. This technique works with both short and long casts. After the cast is made, the rod is held at about shoulder level nearly parallel with the water. As the fly drifts downstream, raise the entire rod to keep the line from bellying. Follow the fly through the drift with good line control and not much if any slack in the line up to

HIGH-STICK WET FLY

1 High-stick nymphing is performed by first making a cast up and across stream. A tuck cast is a good one because the fly will achieve a deep drift immediately. After the fly enters the water, if necessary, remove slack from the line.

2 Lead the wet fly through the drift keeping the tip parallel or slightly ahead of the fly and raising the rod slowly to keep the line from bellying in the current.

3 When the fly passes alongside, slowly begin to lower the rod but don't drop the rod tip.

4 Keep lowering to the rod which adds line to prevent the soft-hackled nymph from dragging and rising to the surface.

5 Lower the rod tip to extend the drift. The fly will begin to swing and rise as the line tightens. You can either let it swing naturally or impart action.

6 The fly swings across the currents. Your rod tip should be pointing at the fly and lower than the rod handle.

the fly. You want the drift to be free of drag so don't pull on the fly, but instead let it drift naturally. Holding the most amount of line possible off the water without disturbing the fly will help you accomplish this. When the fly passes directly across stream from you, lower the rod tip to allow more line down onto the water which now extends the drift below you and keeps the fly from dragging. As the fly continues to drift below you lower the rod tip and reach downstream to get all the drift you can before the fly swings at the end of the cast. At this point the fly can be fished with any of the wet-fly swing

methods. Strikes can occur anytime during the drift. Close proximity high-stick nymph fishing is intimate. You will quite often feel or see the trout strike if the water is clear or shallow enough. Since the presentation drift is often short when high-stick nymphing in-close, an angler can cover the water in a very thorough and quick manner.

FLYMPH MENDING SWING

One of my favorite and most effective presentation casts is the flymph mending swing. This cast incorporates line on the water hump mending for both a drag-free

drift and also tight line strategy for working the fly with action. It made using combined presentation tactics consisting of elements of the Atlantic salmon greased-line method, reach cast, hump mending, slack-line introduction, and line manipulation used in concert to achieve dead drifts or rising action of the fly as needed. The versatility of this cast lets the angler choose which mends or line manipulation combinations to make depending on the current velocity and behavior of the natural he is trying to imitate with his soft-hackled wet-fly. To make this presentation, two upstream or downstream hump mends are made

UPSTREAM AND DOWNSTREAM HUMP MENDS

1 The hump mend is performed after the cast is made. Lift the line beyond the rod tip and throw a belly upstream if the water seam close to you is faster than the water nearer the fly.

2 Throw a downstream hump mend if the water seam closer to you is slower than the water nearer the fly.

immediately after the cast lands on the water. A hump mend is similar to an aerial reach mend in that the idea is to extend the drift of the fly by having the fly line dragged a distance before the effect is transmitted to the fly, but instead of making the mend in the air on the cast it is made by flipping line that is already on the water. To make the hump mend, lift the line that is on the water directly in front of the rod tip and throw a belly upstream or downstream. You should not be straightening the line by doing this, but instead be introducing slack as extra amount of line that the currents have to straighten out before pulling the fly. The direction of the mends you throw is determined by the water current situation. If there is a faster water current seam closer to the angler and slower water nearer the fly, the mends are made upstream. However if the closer seam happens to be slower and the water nearer

the fly faster, the mends are made downstream. The idea is to allow the fly time to drift before the current begins to drag the fly line. Just how many line mends need to be made depends on the current velocity and water turbulence. In slower water, two mends made immediately after the cast may be enough. However, as the water becomes faster you may need to make many, six or more, to keep the fly moving naturally at the same speed as the surrounding current. Mends should be made relative to the water that the line is floating on as this is what causes the drag on the fly, not necessarily the current seam that the fly is in, but the current seams that the line is on. Watch how the line is reacting to the current and if you see it is beginning to drag in the slightest make an upstream or downstream hump mend to counteract the influence of the current speed. The current speeds that the line encounters may change

throughout the drift so you need to react ahead of the current's influence on the line. The idea is to introduce the mends as the drift continues so as to not allow the fly to swing across stream as soon. If the fly and line are at the downstream limit before the swing occurs, these mends made during the drift should be made with slack-line added to the line already outside the rod tip either by introducing line by pulling it off the reel or feeding line that is already available to the line hand. Feed the line by making upstream or downstream hump mends determined by the current seems. Most of the time the soft-hackled nymph will benefit from mends to slow the fly down because of the speed of the current. In the situation that the fly needs to swim faster to look alive you can throw a wide downstream mend into the line introducing a belly that will speed the swing of the fly across stream and activate the soft-hackle collar. This technique is

FLYMPH MENDING SWING

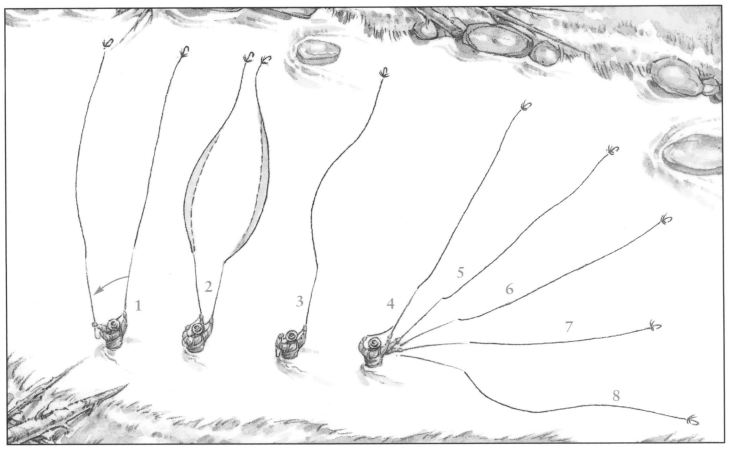

1 Make a cast directly across or down and across stream. If desired, an upstream or downstream reach mend may be made as an initial drag suppressor.

2 After the line lays out, immediately make two upstream or two downstream hump mends. Use upstream mends if there is a faster current seam closer to you and a slower one beyond. Use downstream mends if there is a slower current seam closer to you and a faster one beyond. The idea is to allow the fly to drift further before the fly begins the swing across the current.

3 If you want the fly to drift further in the current lane it's in before the swing begins, you can throw an upstream or downstream mend with slack line that is in your line hand. This introduces extra line that has to be straightened before drag begins and will keep the fly from swinging across stream.

4 Allow the fly to swing across the current. Follow it with your rod tip, lowering the rod tip so the fly swings across and downstream below you.

5 The fly swings across stream. Strikes often come at this point.

6 Continue following the swing with your rod tip, introducing action on the fly if desired.

7 The fly will finish swinging and be hanging in the current below you. You can strip it back towards you with your line hand or release slack line through the rod guides allowing the fly to drift further downstream.

8 A further way to extend the fly presentation and fish out the fly's cast is to reach mend your line across stream to the water that is behind you when the fly is hanging downstream. This will allow a short swing across the water below you and an even longer drift of your fly. Everyone knows that trout aren't caught in the air and the longer you can fish out a cast with a good presentation the more opportunity you allow yourself to be successful and catch a fish.

---

known as the Crosfield draw. This method is good for long runs and pools with little current and where line manipulation would be overkill and result in an unnatural movement of the fly.

Another method to feed line is to shake the rod tip up and down while it is pointed down towards the water. The line will come off the rod with vertical waves. This is a good way to feed line when the fly is downstream of the angler and you want to extend the drift of the fly. The flymph mending swing cast need not be long to be effective. One technique that works particularly well in shallow water is to wade close, fifteen feet or so, and parallel across stream to a spotted or suspected fish lie. Stay low and make your cast close to the fish about two feet above him. Then make one or two immediate upstream or downstream hump mends to allow a

STRIP METHODS

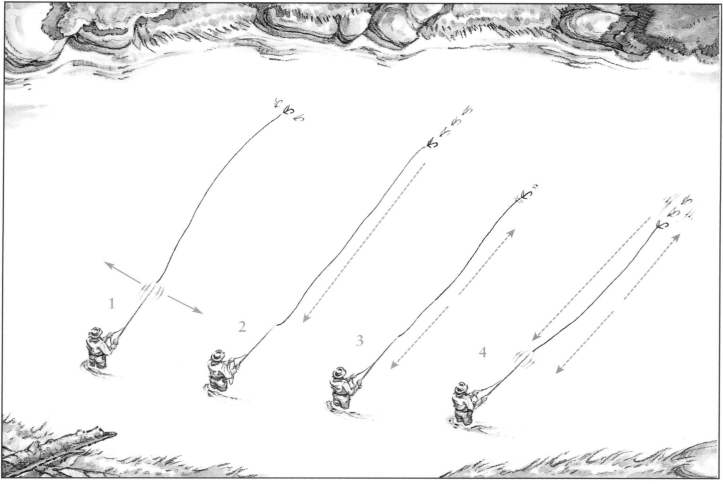

1 Rod-tip twitch left, right or up and down. Make short rod-tip movements.

2 Strip line in.

3 Make short, light pulsating tugs on the fly line with your line hand without stripping or releasing any line.

4 Combine rod-tip twitch with stripping or line tugs.

dragless float. In this situation only the fly needs to be weighted if in shallow water. The drift won't be long and once the fish spots the fly drifting down it often quickly grabs your fly with enthusiasm.

While the wet-fly is drifting you may wish to add movement before or during the current swing. This movement or action can be created in numerous ways. First the line can simply be lifted, causing the fly to ascend towards the surface. Or fly line can be stripped in short or long strokes. Shorter strips, an inch or two, are usually more effective because a little action goes a long way. Also the line can be tugged on which doesn't shorten the drift as stripping does. Make small, light pulsating tugs. Finally you can use the rod

tip to animate the fly by twitching it back and forth or up and down to send a vibration out to the soft-hackled nymph or flymph. Again, this is best done in a moderate or conservative manner. You want the fly to swim like a natural insect. Any of the methods may be combined to form unique presentations.

Instead of concentrating on a floating indicator I use my senses and experience in detecting strikes. In clear, shallow streams I often sight-fish by watching the sideways movement of a trout or the flash of white when one opens its mouth to consume a sub-surface insect. If I'm concentrating and "seeing into the water" I will know where my fly is and strike accordingly. I also watch the end of my fly line or "hot butt" leader for

any pause in the drift, and also tune-into what the rod is telling as a weighted nymph rolling along the stream bottom should be telegraphing its presence. Between these signals I know when to set the hook. Also, since many of these presentations are fished with semi-tight line techniques, strikes can often be felt if you know what to recognize them as. Faint as these strikes may be, you need to learn a high sensitivity to feeling the fish through the fly line. Furthermore, trout often hit these flies hard on the swing. In stream situations where you have to fish with absolutely less drag you simply need to develop the ability to strike at any indication of a fish. As you catch more fish your confidence will increase to the point were you can visualize your fly's drift under water and instinctively know when to use a certain fly, at the right time, in the right place, in the right way. This is what makes a consistently successful fly-fisherman.

Many times I have been fishing a flymph, just below the surface, when at the end of the swing the fish strikes but the hook doesn't set. Instead of stripping the fly in and re-casting I allow the fly to hang there at the location the fish struck and perhaps slightly twitch the rod tip. Oftentimes the fish will re-strike immediately and will usually be hooked the second time. This has happened more times than I can remember, so if you feel that first strike you can almost count on that fish hitting the fly again if you give it the chance. All you have to do is keep the fly within reach.

THE LINE HAND

Instead of holding the line tightly in the line hand next to the rod grip, have extra line already stripped off the reel and draped loosely over the index finger. Holding the line in this fashion and at an angle away from the rod allows you to detect a subtle strike because your line-hand muscles are more relaxed. You can

The line hand.

Line weave.

quickly grasp the line to set the hook and the few feet of extra line on the water behind your line hand is conveniently available for feeding through the guides to extend the drift and allowing for mending.

Another line-hand technique that is particularly useful, especially when high-stick nymphing, is to gather up slack-line and maintain control by line-hand weaving. Gather the line in an organized manner by wrapping the line around your line-hand's index finger and using the rest of your fingers to hold the line as you continue to gather more with the index finger. I prefer to release the gathered line onto the water as I'm weaving it, but I never fully let go of the fly line that's held by my index finger. Taking up the slack will keep you in touch with the nymph, allowing only the minimum amount of line between you and the fly, and limiting drag from line bellying.

EXTENDING DRIFT IN A CURRENT LANE

There is an efficient way to extend the fly's downstream drift in a current lane before allowing it to swing across stream. First gather a sufficient amount of line in loops in your line hand. The more you can hold without it tangling will enable you to extend a longer drift. Two or more loops will be sufficient. Hold the loops in your line hand in a manner that will allow them to be released through the rod guides smoothly. Next, cast across stream into the intended current seam and above the suspected or known fish. As the fly drifts downstream, release each loop of line into the drift with an upstream or downstream hump mend depending on the current seams between you and the fly. Feed the line out at a rate so that the mends hold the fly in the same current lane. Release the line before any drag sets in that could cause the fly to swing. When the fly reaches the point where you want it to swing across stream releasing line. Strikes can come at any point. Be ready.

There are many options for the leaders used for these presentations. For deeper-fished soft-hackled nymphs I prefer to use an 8'11" nymphing leader designed by Joe Humphreys. It is designed to be used with the tuck cast and this leader will help in executing this technique. The tippet is ordinarily around 26", but can be lengthened out to three feet if the water is

very clear and you want the fly further from the line. This leader is used for sub-surface presentations and can be fished un-weighted or weighted with split shot placed on the tippet 8"-18" up from the fly. The distance of the split shot is determined by how close you want the wet-fly to ride near the bottom. For a deep bottom ride, place the split shot 8" above the fly and use a either a bead thorax soft-hackled nymph or one weighted with a lead underbody. If you desire the fly to ride higher off the stream bottom, use an un-weighted soft-hackled nymph and move the split shot up the leader. The split shot is not only useful for getting the wet-fly to the bottom but, is also valuable for slowing down the drift of the fly. The current can drag a fly faster than a natural would drift because of the current's influence on the fly line. In order to make the artificial drift in a natural way you need to use line mends, leader weight, or a combination of both. Split shot comes in various size weights and choices of material, such as lead or tin. I usually start with one BB tin shot and add another if I need to get deeper or if the current is very fast. These two shots combined with a weighted fly, leader mending and the tuck cast will get you a deep bottom drift in almost any water situation. If the fly is dragging through the drift add a split shot to slow it down. In shallow water of a foot or less, a weighted wet-fly alone will usually suffice.

You can also fish more than one wet-fly if you like. Build a dropper as an extension of the tippet blood knot between .008 and .007 using the .008 monofilament for the dropper. The advantages of a dropper fly are that you can fish two levels of water at the same time and double your chances of hooking a trout. A good setup for doing this is to use a weighted soft-hackled nymph as the dropper and an un-weighted flymph as the point fly. The weighted fly will be presented to fish on the bottom and the un-weighted fly will drift in a higher current level as an emerger. The longer the tippet out to the point fly, the higher it will ride. Start with 26" and shorten or lengthen the tippet to get the drift level you desire. If the current is dragging the flies up to the surface, use split shot on the leader 12"-18" back from the point fly.

During emergence, many mayfly nymphs and caddisfly pupae ascend to the surface before fully shedding their shucks. As the mayfly and caddis pupae are shedding their nymphal shucks there is a thin film of air that is caught beneath the shuck. In addition, the unfolding wings have water resistance that creates small bubbles of air due to hydrofuge. Hidy states that, "suggesting these hatching insects with the delicate film or bubble of air takes us beyond the conventional wisdom and into the world of mimicry." He goes on to say, "when properly tied, such flymphs mimic the film of air or the bubble of air that trout see during the insects' metamorphosis."

Fishing flymphs in the film or just under the surface must be done in a way that imitates these natural emergers. The closer trout are feeding to the surface the more selective they can be. In selective feeding situations you must put the fly close to the fish's, rise right in their feeding lane. They will not move very far to take a fly. When the mature nymphs begin emerging to the surface, trout key in on these sub-surface life stages because they are defenseless. A good way to imitate this behavior in the mayflies is to use a fly like the Transition Flymph. First, cast a few feet upstream of the rising fish to allow the fly to sink a little. Then swing the fly in front of the fish using a wet-fly swing or use a mending technique for less drag and a natural float. The fly should appear like a rising natural the fish.

I like to use a relatively long leader with a long tippet for fishing a flymph. My main leader is a George Harvey design. The standard leader is 12' long and has a tippet section of 30". The tippet is only a starting point and can be extended to get more S-curves out to the fly. As far as the tippet diameter is concerned I like to match the diameter to the size fly I am using. Fly size should determine tippet size because a smaller fly will be able to achieve a more subtle drift if a finer tippet is used allowing for a more delicate presentation. A heavier tippet on a small fly can cause the fly to look larger than it is. I use a standard clinch knot on most of my wet-fly connections however I also like the George Harvey dry-fly knot for fishing the flymph as this knot doesn't add any bulk to the hook eye.

In addition, a superb connection for the fly to tippet is the Duncan loop knot. The reason this is such a great knot to use, particularly in slow-moving, clear water, is that it enables the fly to "hang" freely onto the tippet rather than being anchored tightly. The benefit is that the fly will appear un-connected to anything as it is free to move about. This will give the nymph even more of a lifelike quality. This free movement of the fly is especially important when fishing to sophisticated, highly pressured trout. Many spring creek or slow-moving water conditions call for a drag-free, natural drift and the Duncan loop connection greatly helps in this regard. Additionally, the knot is very strong and won't increase the appearance of the fly's size, which is particularly important on small flies, as the knot itself isn't tightened against the eye of the hook. Recently, while fishing the technical waters

DOWNSTREAM PARACHUTE CAST

CURRENT ⟶

1 Face downstream toward the fish. Make a standard backcast.

2 Begin the forward cast.

3 When the line straightens out on the forward cast pull back on the rod tip until the rod is vertical.

4 Lower the rod tip slowly or quickly depending on the current speed. You want to allow the fly to drift downstream at the same speed that the current is traveling.

5 Continue to lower the rod tip as the fly drifts into the fish's feeding lie.

SLACK-LINE CAST

1 Make a standard overhead backcast.

2 Begin the forward casting stroke. When the rod reaches 10:00 check the cast.

3 When the line has nearly straightened out on the forward cast, drop the rod's level by lowering your elbow about six inches without changing the angle of the rod.

4 Lower the rod tip. The line will unfurl and layout on the water. The leader should have S-curves in it up to the fly. If necessary, lengthen the tippet until it allows the leader to fall in S-curves.

---

of Silver Creek, I found the Duncan loop performed better in providing a natural looking behavior of a Pheasant Tail Soft-Hackle in imitating emerging pale morning duns. On Silver Creek, late in the season, when #18 or #20 PMD's are hatching I recommend fishing a small #20 Pheasant Tail Soft-Hackle . This fly is what I often catch the majority of my fish with on many streams. The reason is that a Pheasant Tail Soft-Hackle imitates 99% of all mayfly nymphs and a #20 in particular is a commonly small nymph size in many moving waters. The small size coupled with its convincing imitation of a natural make it the deadliest fly ever.

The hydrofuge or film of air present on fur-bodied soft-hackled nymphs is important in matching the natural's emerging water-resistant wings. When imitating emergers just under the surface you'll want a dry, fresh soft-hackled flymph so that when the fly is pulled under water the fur will hold air and create the impression of the unfolding wings of the

natural. If you are interested in imitating less mature nymphs on the stream-bed you'll not be concerned with the hydrofuge. In this case, in order to make the un-weighted nymph sink quicker hold the fly under water and squeeze it. This will allow the fly to absorb water helping to keep it drifting at a deeper level under the surface. Mending the line to keep it from dragging is also often necessary in keeping the fly submerged and drifting at a proper level.

DOWNSTREAM PARACHUTE CAST

For fishing the emerging flymphs you need to use some dry-fly tactics. Usually I like to fish the flymphs downstream to the fish. This keeps the line and leader above the fish and out of their sense of vision. This way the fish sees the fly first and this is important when the fish are sophisticated and have seen a lot of presentations. A cast using a slack-line presentation, such as the

downstream parachute cast, will work well. The parachute cast is made by casting the line down towards the target, but before the line lands on the forward cast pull back on the rod tip which causes the line to belly in a vertical reach cast. Then slowly lower the rod tip to feed line downstream keeping pace with the current and allowing your fly to drift into the fish without drag.

SLACK-LINE CAST

George Harvey designed his dry-fly leader to be used in conjunction with the slack-line cast to achieve drag-free drifts with of dry flies. The leader and the cast can also be applied to fishing flymphs just under the surface or in the film. The slack-line cast is another cast that uses a rod check to achieve a desired effect on the fly line. In this case the rod check allows the leader to fall in S-curves that have to be straightened by the current before the fly begins to drag. This ingenious cast

REACH MEND

1 Make the cast toward the target.

2 As the line straightens out on the forward cast, make a reach mend either to the side of your casting arm or across your body. Fish out the drift with your method of choice.

addresses prolonging a drag-free drift by using slack in the leader instead of slack in the fly line, which is where the attention should be focused because although you might have slack in the fly line, the fly could still be dragging due to a straight leader. You don't want a straight leader for drag-free surface fishing. The longer it takes to straighten the leader the longer your fly has a chance to drift without drag. This idea is at the heart of the cast and leader design. In addition to the cast and leader you need to lengthen the tippet until the S-curves are pronounced enough. Test-cast the leader with the fly attached and watch how the S-curves develop in it. If they are not as evident as they should be

with a proper slack-line cast add a longer tippet until the S-curves are slack enough. Begin the slack-line cast by making a standard overhead backcast. As you make the forward cast apply power using the thumb and a squeeze of the rod grip. As the line is unloading forward, check the cast by stopping the rod abruptly at 10:00 then drop your elbow along with the rod but keep the rod in the 10:00 position while lowering your arm level. Finally, lower the rod tip down to the water. The rod check should send out S-curves into your leader. This cast and leader combination will give you a surface drag-free drift better than any other system. A good situation to use this cast is when you

are fishing a Hare's Ear Soft-Hackle as a spent caddisfly in the surface film and wish to achieve a drag-free float from your artificial.

REACH MEND

Another very important line-mending technique and one that can be incorporated into any wet-fly cast is a reach mend. This mend is performed before any line falls to the water. It will not interfere with any of these casts since it can be incorporated into them as preferred. To perform this cast after you make the forward cast and before the line falls to the water, simply reach the rod out to your casting arm side or reach the rod across your body to the opposite side. The line coming off the rod tip on the forward cast will lay out to either side and have to be dragged by the currents for the length of the reach before the line begins to belly. The reach mend can be performed in any casting direction, across stream, upstream, or downstream. It is the most employed method I use for reducing drag if there are varying speed current seams between the fly and me.

Soft-hackled nymph presentations are designed to activate the fly's body material and hackle in the current, thus imitating the movement of the natural. Small amounts of drag from can actually be used to an advantage in fast or slow-moving water because as insects emerge they frequently move across currents, particularly many of the caddis species pupae, as they are good swimmers. These wet flies are usually most effective when fished so as to animate the fibers of the fly, i.e. in a way as Leisenring suggested up and across, across stream, down and across, or straight downstream. These presentations allow the fly to have maximum animation with the soft-hackle fibers pulsating and breathing.

We know that flymphs are particularly useful for imitating the emerging stages of Ephemeroptera (mayfly), Trichoptera (caddisfly), and Diptera (midge). But they are not limited to being fished as emerging invertebrates. An example is in the case of spent caddisflies where flymphs such as the Hare's Ear Soft-Hackle fished on the surface in various body shades are very good imitations of egg-laying caddisflies. When trout are feeding on adult mayflies (sub-imagos) I will sometimes use standard dry-fly patterns such as Comparaduns, paraloops, thorax duns, no hackles, or parachutes. However, at times of selective feeding during a hatch, emergers are almost always preferred by trout because of this stage's vulnerability and thus flymphs work even when you see trout feeding on adult naturals.

Now let's talk about mayfly spinners (imagos). Commonly dry flies like Z-Lon Wing Spinners, CDC or Parachute Biot Spinners work well, but flymphs are so versatile that they also can imitate spent mayflies and, as we'll see later, ovipositing caddis. Un-weighted flymph patterns, such as the Ascension Flymph, Blue Dun, Honey Dun, Diving Baetis Spinner, Little Olive Flymphs, Pale Watery Dun Wingless, Sulphur Wingless, and the Tup's Nymph, all

have dubbed bodies that can be matched in size and color to imitate particular mayfly natural spinners. To fish a flymph on the surface as a spinner apply a sparse amount of floatant to the hackle collar, body, and tail of the flymph. Tye the flymph sparse and fish it completely dead drift. The hackle collar will lay spread out on the water surface and appear very similar to the clear, lightly veigned wings of the natural. The flymph may even appear as a spinner whose wings are broken or torn. Furthermore, the flymph can be fished without fly floatant under the surface to imitate a sunk or diving egg-laying spinner. This overlooked and under-fished technique can be killer because dead, spent spinners don't drift on the surface forever. Eventually their bodies lose buoyancy or become washed under by the current where they are easy food for trout.

When hooking a trout on a downstream cast, it's important to use sharp hooks. Because the angle of the hookset on a downstream cast is actually away from the fish back towards the fisherman, many times the fish isn't hooked as well as during an upstream presentation where the hook is set into the fish's mouth. To better set the hook when fishing downstream, use a slip strike or a slight lift of the rod tip as the current can help you drive the hook in if you don't overreact on your strike. The slip strike is performed by simply letting go of the fly line in the line hand and then immediately lifting the tip of the rod which allows the line to "slip" through the guides. The slip strike doesn't move the fly very much which is absolutely necessary for hooking a fish in these situations. Don't strike by tugging on the line because doing this will probably pull the hook out of the mouth and away from the fish. After the hook is set if you play the fish using side pressure from a horizontally held rod you have a greater mechanical advantage than a rod that is held vertical allowing you turn and land the fish quicker. Side pressure also helps keep the hook set in the trout's jaw. While side pressure is the best way to quickly tire and land a fish it works best in water that doesn't have large amounts of aquatic vegetation. In spring-creek-type environments where in-stream vegetation can fill the stream from the bottom to the surface, it's best to play fish with a high rod tip to keep the fish's head up and not allow to dive into the weeds. It's often worth it to take a chance of having the hook pull out rather than letting a trout dive into heavy vegetation and breaking the tippet or

dislodging the hook. Decide on which technique would be most successful before making the cast. This preparation allows you to have a game plan.

If the fish is large and is using the current to its advantage, try to get below or alongside the fish while you are playing it. If the water conditions allow you to wade downstream and get below the trout make sure that you move cautiously to keep the fish on the line and to avoid spooking the fish that you haven't caught yet. Moving downstream may be worth it to get a better angle on the large fish you have on. Wade slowly as you move downstream maintaining line tension and using side pressure. When you get alongside or below the fish continue to play it using side pressure until you are able to land it. Trout can build up large amounts of lactic acid when they are being played by the angler, so the faster you land the fish the less oxygen is depleted by their muscles allowing them to recover more quickly. Support the fish by cradling it in the water to allow it to recover and make sure it has recovered sufficiently before release.

Here is a tip to help you prepare for when the fish are being very selective and you have to make a technical presentation. First relax. Then visualize your cast and any mending you will need to make. You should know where your fly will land and the path it will take on its drift. Next take a slow deep breath and exhale. When you know the presentation you will make then make your cast.

Leaders are an often under-appreciated piece of equipment but a correctly tapered leader will give you presentation subtleties that will give your fly an advantage. In order for the fish to believe that your fly is a natural it must behave like there is no leader connected to it at all. This, as we have discussed, is achieved through a combination of proper leader, weight, casting, and mending choices. When fishing un-weighted, soft-hackled emergers on an un-weighted leader up to about a foot or less under the water surface, it's beneficial to treat the leader with a leader sink agent to remove residual grease and add a film of "weight" so that the leader sinks and aids in keeping the fly from buoying up to the surface. There are many commercial products designed to achieve this such as Orvis Mud, Loon Outdoors Snake River Mud, and Fuller's Earth compound applied to the full length of the leader. Not only does treating a leader in this fashion help

The slip strike is made by releasing the line from the line hand while simultaneously raising the rod tip allowing the line to "slip" through the guides. The tension of the line against the rod provides a delicate hook-set.

the fly break the surface tension and sink, it also removes unwanted glare from the monofilament. When fishing in crystal-clear, flat-water conditions, removing leader glare to further disguise the leader is an especially important factor in making stealthy presentations to highly sensitive and selective trout.

Customarily British anglers have used Fuller's Earth to sink and conceal their leaders. This traditional leader sink paste is made from a mixture of Fuller's Earth, dishwashing soap, and glycerin. A conveniently available source of Fuller's Earth is common cat litter which contains the same clay compound found in Fuller's Earth and can be made into a powder by putting a small amount in a plastic bag and using a hammer to grind it into a powder. To the powder gradually add a small amount of dishwashing soap until it becomes a stiff paste. Storing the leader sink paste in a 35mm film canister will keep it moist. If the paste begins to dry out adding a little water will re-moisturize it.

If you find yourself on the water without any leader sink, a pinch of thick, clay-like stream bank mud applied to the leader will sink it temporarily, as well as take the glare off the monofilament.

In addition to leader sink compounds I also use a leader straightener to remove glare from the tippet. This results in the tippet material refracting less light and also helps to sink the tippet slightly under water. Used correctly a leader straightener

microscopically scores the monofilament and allows the tippet to sink slightly easier. Take care to only pull the straightener once across the tippet section of the leader, just enough to dull the finish and remove the glare. When used in this manner I have not found that the leader straightener causes any damage that results in broken tippets. These leader sink and concealment methods will help the un-weighted fly stay under water easier and lessen the shadow the leader throws on the stream bottom.

I would like to close this presentation discussion with some thoughts on casting distances. Making a relatively long cast using wet flies can have advantages. Wet-fly swing casts seem to allow the fly to swing in a more appealing fashion if the cast is at least thirty-five to forty-five feet, or in some cases even more. A further

benefit of a longer cast is that you are outside of the fishes window and they can't detect your presence as easily. This fact, in conjunction with a downstream presentation, further allows you to become "invisible" which can only benefit your chances of catching more fish. A longer cast also gives your fly a chance at being exposed to more potentially hungry fish as the drift and swing covers more feeding lies. However this is not to say that every cast should be long. I like to fish a stream on a case-by-case basis. I first read the water close to me and fish it thoroughly before extending my casts. Don't wade unnecessarily, fish the water carefully before you move on. Above all remember to think like a predator. Fish methodically and with purpose. Be like the heron that unhurriedly stalks the fish.

High-stick nymphing has many advantages. It keeps minimal line off the water which decreases fly drag, strikes can be noticed or felt easier because of less line slack, hook-sets can be quicker because the angler is in close contact with the fly, and it complements the tuck cast. Notice the extra line behind my line hand that I can feed out to extend the drift.

Baetis Nymph

Chapter Five

FISHING SITUATIONS &
Fly Selection

Now that we have discussed the casts, presentations and the fly-tying aspects of these specific wet flies, we will address the final and arguably most important factor, which fly to use and when to use it. There are three basic criteria for determining which fly to use:

1 The water type and stream conditions: *speed, depth, water clarity.*

2 The fish's feeding behavior: *if the fish are rising or feeding sub-surface.*

3 The most abundant food form: *mayfly, caddisfly, midge, or other.*

You need to first analyze the on-stream conditions before choosing any leader or fly. The choice of the fly and the way in which it will be fished are relative to the answers to the above criteria.

WATER TYPES

Trout waters include a variety of coldwater streams that vary widely in their water quality and fertility. Among these are freestone streams, tailwater streams, spring creeks, and freestone streams with spring-water contributions. Trout streams also vary in depth. Some are relatively consistent in their water depth and current speed while others have many types of water such as shallow runs, deep holes, glassy flats and quick pocket-water seams. Soft-hackled nymphs can be fished in all types of water, but depending on the conditions you need to use different presentation methods, as well as the appropriate pattern, to have the most success.

Freestone streams can be wonderful waters in which to fish these flies. The faster water riffle sections activate the soft-hackle fibers even without line manipulation. Freestone streams are predominantly fed by tributaries that gather their water through ground runoff

from rain or snowmelt. Some of these streams also have spring-water contributions that help stabilize their temperature and depth. In order to locate fish and be able to predict how they could be feeding you need to be aware of the streams' seasonal life cycles and the conditions that affect them. Freestone streams come in many forms with some streams being more fertile than others.

Freestone water quality is very much subject to environmental factors. During drought conditions the freestone streams suffer from low water flows and higher water temperatures that cause stress on the fish. Aquatic insects too can lose habitat in low water which reduces the food base.

The water might be 75° in the summer, which is at the upper end of a trout's survival limit, and could fall to less than 40° or even freezing over in places in the winter. The swing in water temperatures between the summer and the winter changes the fishes' metabolism to the point where their feeding routine is disrupted. These water temperature changes create times when the fish are more opportunistic in feeding. In order to understand what you can expect of the fish from the conditions present you need to take the water temperature in trout streams, especially in freestone streams. Carry a stream thermometer with you at all times and use it. Water temperatures between

Lifting the rod tip slightly at the end of the drift will cause the flymph to rise to the surface quicker and can excite a trout into making an "induced take".

Spring creeks offer the most stable trout habitat.

55°-65° are most ideal for locating feeding trout. As we discuss later, temperatures outside this range have quite an effect on the fish. This ten-degree range is the not only the most comfortable to the fish, but also sees the most insect activity, particularly among most mayfly and caddisfly species.

Spring creeks and tailwaters can for the most part be considered similar water conditions. These waters are generally not as subject to the fluctuations that freestone streams face. The water conditions are much more evenly regulated as the water is either fed from underground aquifers or deep reservoirs. They have consistent water levels and cfs flows, the exception being during hydroelectric generation on tailwaters and extreme drought on spring creeks. The water temperature throughout the year doesn't change more than 5°-10° on most spring creeks which can help to keep the fishes' metabolism consistent throughout the year. However in late summer the fully grown aquatic vegetation can have an effect on the dissolved oxygen content. You see plants give off oxygen through photosynthesis during sunlight hours, however at night the plants are not producing oxygen, but rather involved in respiration which consumes oxygen from the water. Dissolved oxygen levels are at their lowest immediately before dawn and rise throughout the daylight hours.

As these waters have their sources below ground many impurities found in freestone streams are non-existent in spring-fed streams. The water as it flows through the limestone is both filtered and receives minerals from the rocks. The limestone spring creeks have a more stable pH which leans toward alkaline. The stable pH levels promote tremendous quantities of aquatic weed growth providing a platform of food and shelter

Biot & Peacock.

Pete Hidy was very successful in fishing them on Silver Creek, a stream with some of the most sophisticated rainbow and brown trout in the world.

Approaching trout close enough to get a good presentation can be difficult in shallow, clear water. The water clarity provides a chance for the trout to get a good visual on both the under water. conditions and what's going on above the surface as well. The trout will be able to detect any food in the water as well as any predators above the stream including anglers. The deeper the fish is under water, the larger their window is on the surface and above the water. You need to position yourself to make a well-executed cast while remaining invisible to the fish so you don't send them scurrying for cover or put them down from feeding. Make sure you

for the biomass of stream. Insect life flourishes because of this and these plants also offer the trout feeding lies and cover. The fish in these fertile waters usually have a higher amount of food to choose from as a result. The fact that food is more abundant affords fish the luxury of being more selective as a defensive mechanism. They can afford to pass up a food item if it's suspicious as another one will be arriving in their feeding lie soon. Think of it as protection through selection. The slower drift of the natural due to current speed as well as water clarity also allows for discriminating inspection of the food item. While the water often looks similar, spring creeks have many variable water currents because of the way the aquatic plants channel the water. This can cause the drag on a fly to be considerable making it very difficult to get a drag-free float. One way to get a good drag-free presentation is to use a downstream cast, along with the mending techniques and leader design talked about in the Presentation Strategies chapter.

Flymphs that are fished in spring creeks have to be very close in design and behavior to the naturals. I like using a sparser pattern for spring creeks where the fish have longer to scrutinize the fly. Oliver Kite, the talented nymph fisherman, took minimalism to the extreme. Kite often fished his Bare Hook Nymph which is merely a hook dressed with a dozen or so wraps of copper wire colored to match the insect's thorax. Kite even used bare hooks

Brown trout and #16 Bukcheon Spider.

by themselves to simulate mayfly nymphs and was renowned for his ability to catch fish using these minimal tactics. He also used the Sawyer Pheasant Tail Nymph in various sizes for a great deal of his nymphing. For mayfly flymph patterns in flat, clear water I prefer to use sparse flymphs like the Transition Flymph or a Pheasant Tail SHN with or without a trailing shuck. However for caddisfly pupae I will use a slightly heavier dressed pattern like the Emerald Caddis. For those who might question the effectiveness of the buggier impressionism of a flymph on a flat spring creek I must point out that

keep a low profile. Wear camouflage if necessary and blend in with the surroundings. Use trees or bushes to conceal yourself and stay low. If possible, on small streams stay out of the water entirely and cast from the bank. This will keep you from causing any disturbance to the water currents or stream structure which will alert the fish to your presence. Sound travels very fast through water and walking over rocks while wading calls attention to yourself if the water doesn't have any turbulence to mask the sounds caused by a wading angler.

Also be cautious when walking near

A stealthy downstream presentation is paramount in technical spring creek situations.

the banks. Many streams have undercut banks and walking on them is basically like walking on top of a fish's living room. When fishing to the spookiest fish from the bank it may be necessary to kneel down or even lie down in your casting position to remain invisible. Quite often, flat water is where we will find rising fish. There are several reasons for this. Since the current flow in flat water is usually slower than surrounding runs or riffles a fish can hold under the surface and intercept naturals without expending too much energy. These areas too hold challenging fishing for these are the areas where many of the mayfly and midge species most often hatch. The surface doesn't have as much distortion as riffle water does allowing the fish to inspect the naturals more closely. Whether on spring creeks, tailwaters, or freestone streams, if there is going to be surface rise activity it will often be found in the flat-water sections between faster water sections. Shallow, flat water of four feet or less usually provides the best opportunity to find rising fish. For the

most part trout like to rise in shallower water because they feel more comfortable as it provides more security from predators that attack from below. Shallower water allows the trout to get to the bottom and find protective shelter in the weeds or under water. structure quicker. This is not to say that trout in deeper water won't feed on the surface, but you will find them feeding on the surface more often in flat water of four feet or less. Even with all of the challenge of fishing for trout in these technical situations, the good news is that this is often sight-fishing meaning that you can spot the fish and watch its reaction to your presentation.

At the other extreme, turbid water that is a little off color from rain runoff can still be fished with the right wet fly. Common sense says that you will need to make your fly easier for the fish to spot. This can be done through size, color, design, or a combination of these elements. Using a fly that has a light shade of fur or a bright bead thorax is one

approach. Also using a larger soft-hackled nymph for fishing in off-color water can help the fish to locate the fly. Many times this means going deep with a slow drift to have a shot at a fish. I will use a weighted leader and a large #10 or #12 weighted fly such as an Orange Hare Wingless or a bright fly like the Partridge & Chartreuse. You will need to fish the water slowly and thoroughly giving the fish every opportunity to strike your fly. This is a good situation in which to use a dropper fly as it doubles your chances of drawing a fish's attention and a strike.

Faster water stream sections like riffles and pocket-water are great places to fish soft-hackled nymphs. They almost seem custom made for them. The action of the currents play on the soft-hackle fibers making them come alive, even without the angler's assistance. The hackle's life-imparting fibers can look very appetizing to trout under these conditions. Fish in riffles and pocket-water are more opportunistic than those in slower, flat-water stream sections because they have to make a quick decision on whether or not to take food items. They don't have a lot of time to think about it as the food travels quickly downstream. With this said, these fish can still sometimes be particular to the size, shape, and color of the artificial fly depending on the water level, so it's a good idea to carry a few different sizes in any fly to find the one which will suit the trout on a particular day.

I love fishing small mountain headwater streams for trout. The fish are sometimes small, but they are wild and

extremely valuable. While I was living in Korea I would often travel to Gangwon province and fish for the native cherry trout that live in the swift, pocket-water streams of the Taeback Mountains. These fish are difficult to catch when the water is low, requiring careful stalking and presentation methods. While fishing there I found that traditional North Country spiders like the Partridge and Green were very effective, but at times lacked sufficient ability to float and would sink too quickly in the water when fished

upstream on the surface. I also wanted a more visible soft-hackle wet fly that I could fish on the surface. In this regard I invented the Bukcheon Spider, named after Bukcheon, one of the finest cherry trout streams in the province. This fly incorporates two soft-hackles. One is a rear hackle collar of CDC. The CDC hackle floats the fly for a long time in the surface film even in rough, turbulent pocket-water and also adds visibility making the fly easier to detect. In front of the CDC is a soft-hackle collar of gray partridge. The Bukcheon Spider is meant to be fished upstream in the fashion of the North Country wet-fly patterns. This pattern floats well without any dressing due to the CDC rear hackle collar. It rides with the hackle both in the surface film and on top of the surface and is very visible in pocket-water currents. Riffle water also provides one of the most effective fly/presentation tactics for matching emerging caddis pupae. First, use a bead thorax Hare's Ear SHN or un-weighted Hare's Ear SHN of the appropriate shade and cast above the fish. Then use a Leisenring Lift as the fly approaches the fish to imitate the surface-bound pupae and trigger a strike. For this presentation I would use the Humphrey's nymph leader and a tippet of 30" to allow the fly to have more action in the current.

The tuck cast drives the nymph into the water allowing the nymph to gain depth readily.

FISHING DEPTH

There is a saying that goes, "the difference between a good nymph fisherman and a great nymph fisherman is one split shot." Your fly has to be presented at the depth, the fish are holding. This level can vary with stream depth, but remember that for a fish to have to swim to the surface every time they needed a food item would consume too much energy and would be inefficient. As a result, trout will not travel too far to eat the food item, especially if it's a small payback in caloric intake. It is essential that you present the food at their feeding zone in the water column. This may be near the surface or near the bottom of the stream because these zones hold the most amount of natural food sources. The middle zone is more of a transition zone for the naturals. The food is not as concentrated in this zone and thus it is less efficient for the fish to expend energy here to find caloric nourishment. As in surface dry-fly fishing, the sub-surface fly must

Building weight into the fly is necessary when the fish are feeding deep or in swift current.

travel with the drift at the same rate as the naturals. In order to accomplish this weight on the leader and built into the fly is very often necessary. When fishing sub-surface in fast-water currents you need to use split shot on the leader to slow the fly's drift down. Otherwise the current water will pull the fly along too fast creating drag and an unnatural looking fly. The weight not only slows down the drift, but it also keeps the wet-fly from buoying up to the surface until you want it to. Upstream or downstream hump mends or reach mends also will allow for a longer natural drift. The wet-fly swing benefits from the split shot in fast water in that the soft-hackled nymph will still rise to top on the , but will do so at a slower, more natural rate. Here is a list of the methods used to weight the soft-hackled wet flies from lightest to heaviest.

PHEASANT TAIL FLYMPH *(un-weighted)*

The lightest weight flymphs for surface, or just under the surface, are non-fur-bodied flymphs like the Pheasant Tail Flymph and the B&P. These will not sink very far and are good for imitating floating or emerging nymphs.

FUR-BODIED FLYMPH *(un-weighted)*

A slightly heavier weight. These will sink a little easier after holding and squeezing them under water. to allow the fly to become saturated.

FLYMPH, GLASS BEAD THORAX

A flymph with a glass-bead thorax is good for shallow, clear water where you don't need a deep drift but want the fly to sink inches under the surface. The glass beads don't reflect a lot of light and are aesthetically non-threatening to the fish.

SOFT-HACKLED NYMPH WITH A LEAD-WIRE UNDERBODY

A medium-weight wet-fly is the lead-wire underbody nymph. These use either .010, .015, or .020 lead wire depending on hook size. The weight can be varied on them with the number of wraps around the hook shank, but try to keep the lead underbody in the thorax area of the fly. A wet-fly weighted with lead on the front half of the fly will ride with the hook-eye up and produces a sort of jigging action if dead drifted along the bottom. Weighted wet flies will ride upside down with the hook bend up due to the weight on the hook shank flipping the fly over. However this doesn't effect the appearance of the fly as the flies have symmetry at any angle because they are tied without specific top or bottom features. If you want the fly to ride right-side up with the hook point down, weight the fly in the front half of the hook shank and then flatten the lead wire parallel to the ground.

SOFT-HACKLED NYMPH WITH A BRASS OR COPPER BEAD THORAX

The next heaviest weight is the bead-thorax flies. Copper and brass beads weigh slightly more relative to an equivalent amount of lead wire. They also provide a bit of flash which can catch a fish's attention.

SOFT-HACKLE NYMPH WITH A TUNGSTEN BEAD THORAX

The heaviest weight of nymph is accomplished by using a tungsten bead for the thorax. Tungsten beads weigh more than twice the amount of similar size copper or brass beads.

The Orient Express is a tungsten bead thorax nymph that is good for deep, fast current. It is further weighted by wrapping the amber copper wire, used for the ribbing, tightly around the shank underneath the pheasant-tail fibers. This fly is heavy enough that it will sink and drift on the bottom often without split shot allowing the angler to "guide" it through seductive-looking feeding lanes and feel strikes when high-stick nymphing.

Use this as a guide to help you tie weight into your artificials and also to help you decide on the wet-fly to use based on how deep it needs to be fished. Split shot in combination with a weighted fly may be necessary to get to the fish's feeding depth or slow the fly down in fast current.

When the water currents are not as strong or a shallow sub-surface presentation is desired, un-weighted flymphs are very effective. If the water is less than two feet and not too fast, an un-weighted flymph can be fished sub-surface with only line mending needed for a bottom-to-top presentation. In this case, I might use a glass-bead thorax flymph. The advantage of using a weighted fly alone, when the conditions allow it, is the fact that the closer the weight is to the fly, in this case built into the fly, the less noticeable it is when casting.

THE NATURALS

I have found that even though soft-hackled wet flies were originally designed to imitate emerging mayfly, caddisfly and stonefly species they can be tied to imitate any sub-surface aquatic insect. Some will ask how a fly with a soft-hackle collar imitates a nymphal insect form. I answer this by stating that the soft-hackles can be taken as an imitation of nymphal legs or simply animated movement, indicating life. The greatest confirmation to using them as nymph imitations however is that the fish find them attractive and you can't argue with that. By employing different sizes and presentations the playing field is wide open into their use.

EPHEMEROPTERA: *Mayflies*

Mayflies have long been a favored insect

Ascension Flymph.

for imitation by fly-fisherman. Dry-fly fishing using adult mayfly patterns is arguably an easier form of fly-fishing, at least from a visual perspective. You are able to spot a rising fish and track the presentation of your fly, seeing the fish's reaction and knowing when to strike. It's all above water, plainly visible to the angler. However, often what anglers think are trout rising to adult mayflies actually are head and tail rises to sub-surface nymphs or emergers in the film. This is where flymphs come in and here is why they do a very good job of imitating the appearance of life in mayfly nymphs and emergers. As the mayfly nymph matures under water. the nymphal shell fills with gasses that will raise the fly to the surface when the nymph is mature and ready to emerge into an adult. As the nymph rises, the nymphal shell holds gas bubbles on the outside as well. All of these small gas bubbles reflect light and make these nymphs very attractive to fish. A flymph's dubbed-fur body and soft-hackle fibers help to trap air and actually hold air bubbles just like the naturals. This is what Hidy refers to as the hydrofuge. Frank Sawyer, like James Leisenring, was very influenced by G.E.M. Skues' nymphing tactics. Sawyer invented one of the most realistic nymph patterns then or now, the Sawyer Pheasant Tail Nymph. His is the original version of the pheasant-tail nymph and is tied with only pheasant-tail fibers and copper wire. Sawyer designed it originally to imitate Baetis mayfly nymphs. He had observed that the Baetis nymphs held their legs close to their bodies and felt that the pattern sufficiently imitated them without the need for any hackle. It has been copied and many variations have been invented. The American Pheasant Tail Nymph with a peacock thorax is drawn upon for the Pheasant Tail SHN. This soft-hackle nymph pattern is the most successful fly I know for imitating mayfly nymphs. It's my go-to fly for mayfly emergers when fished just inches below the surface and can also be fished deeper for imitating swimming-type mayfly species simply by changing the pattern size and adding weight. In clear, deep water where the fish are holding on the bottom you need extra weight on both the wet-fly and the leader to reach their feeding lanes. For imitation of mayfly nymphs in these situations, again I prefer a weighted Pheasant Tail Soft-Hackle in a size to

Honey Dun flymph.

Blue Dun flymph.

match the naturals often with split shot on the leader to slow the drift down.

While most species of mayfly nymphs are of a predominantly brownish shade, Baetis species are often more olive than brown and an effective variation of a natural shade Pheasant Tail Soft-Hackle nymph is to tie the tail and abdomen with olive pheasant-tail fibers and an olive partridge feather for the soft-hackle collar. Additionally, the shedding shuck for a Baetis Pheasant Tail Flymph can be constructed of mixture of brown and olive

Z-lon fibers. Another pheasant-tail nymph variation, this one to match emerging blue-winged olives just under the surface, is a fly I call the Electric Emerger. It's tied on a heavy 1X long nymph hook in the larger sizes and a light-gauge, dry-fly hook in the smaller sizes. It employs olive pheasant-tail fibers for the tail and abdomen, a green copper wire rib, a peacock herl thorax, and olive mallard flank fibers tied soft-hackle style using a distributed collar wrap.

Other effective sub-surface mayfly

Little Olive Flymph palmered.

Emerald Caddis.

variations. These patterns do a yeoman's job of imitating an emerging or floating mayfly nymph about to transform into an adult. This stage is very often the one that trout key in on. The reason is that this is the most vulnerable point in the life of the mayfly. It is trying to both free itself from its nymphal shuck and break through the surface-water tension. The flymphs soft-hackle fibers extend back over the fly's body and appear as a natural's legs held in close to allow for an aerodynamic shape while rising to the suface. The nymphal shuck can sometimes be difficult for the mayfly to free itself from and the trout don't have to work as hard to catch these naturals making them an attractive target.

Mayflies duns emerge from their nymphal form in one of three different ways. First are the species that emerge into the dun under water. and swim to the surface, another behavior is hanging in the surface film and crawling out of the nymph case, and finally sometimes mayflies crawl out of the water entirely and shed their nymphal shuck while resting on a stone or tree branch on dry land. The exact emergence behavior varies between swimming, crawling, clinging, and burrowing mayfly species. Obviously, species that emerge while in the water are more vulnerable to trout. Ephemerella species like Pale Morning Duns often fully emerge a foot or so under water. and swim to the surface in adult dun form without a nymphal case attached. These subsurface emergences are well imitated by using a Transition Flymph. This fly has the rear abdomen of a nymph and the thorax of a dun with soft-hackle fibers suggesting unfolding wings and legs. To imitate a fully emerged adult mayfly dun swimming to the surface, I use the Ascension Flymph or a Tup's Nymph. These two flies are pale yellow like a natural PMD and have the same characteristics—wings and tail of an adult mayfly.

My standard approach to mayfly emerger fishing is to use a 12' Harvey leader with a long tippet, about four feet. If the stream conditions allow me to I then get into casting position across stream and above the fish. Staying low, I move slow and acquire the best possible location for remaining invisible yet allowing for a good presentation. It's best to be casting across as few cross-currents as possible, so you can maintain good line control and have less variable currents trying to drag the fly

nymph imitations include the Gray Hackle, Iron Blue Dun, Hare's Ear SHN, Whitlock's Red Fox Squirrel-Hair Nymph, Allen's Drake, B&B and the B&P. Use the tuck cast and line mending to get a deep natural drift. I most often use the 8'11" nymph leader or the dropper fly leader when I am fishing the stream bottom and up to a few inches under the surface at which time I will usually switch to a leader designed for surface presentation such as a Harvey 12' taper. It is important to match the tippet diameter to the fly size as well as

its weight including the split shot. A 4X or 5X tippet will work well and sink faster if you're not fishing a large fly or casting heavy split shot.

If you are seeing head and tail rises during a mayfly hatch or very subtle snout rises, and not seeing an adult being taken, the fish are probably feeding on hatching nymphs just under or on the surface. Whether the fish are taking mayfly nymphs on the top or the bottom of the stream my first choice is still one of the soft-hackled pheasant-tail pattern line. The presentation should be a down-and-across flymph mending swing cast or a downstream dead-drift parachute cast. When using induced take methods, a downstream presentation will allow the fibers on the flymph to animate better than an upstream one because the fly's hackle fibers will be held under more tension by the water activating their action. Also you will never line the fish with a downstream cast. The only thing the fish sees is the fly. Quite often an induced take technique will trigger a fish's instinct to take just as the fly reaches the strike zone. Any of the mayfly flymph patterns, such as the Transition Flymph, PMD Ascension Flymph, Honey Dun, Blue Dun Hackle, or the one of the various pheasant-tail flies such as the Pheasant Tail Flymph with trailing shuck, will all do excellent duty as mayfly emerging patterns. If you want to fish the flymph on the surface or in the film, a greased leader can be used to keep the flymph from sinking.

If you want to simulate the mayfly rising to the surface, use an un-greased leader and cast just upstream of the fish to allow the fly to sink a foot or so. Then as the fly begins to swing in front of the fish the flymph will rise to the top with the same motion the natural uses. While not meant to imitate a nymphal form of a mayfly, an often underused but very effective method to fish during the end of the BWO hatch is in imitating the egg-laying spinners. Recently fly-fishermen have begun to pay attention to the importance in a trout's diet of adult female mayfly spinners diving under water. to lay eggs during a spinner fall. This behavior is quite common and when available trout feed on sunken spinners more often than the ones floating spent on the surface. This is an important fact that many anglers should realize and take advantage of. For instance, many species of Baetis

females crawl under water. to lay their eggs and a Diving Baetis Spinner will imitate the mayflies that crawl under water. to lay eggs and are washed away in the current. Other prodigious species like pale morning dun's and sulphurs have spinner falls that can be effectively fished with an Ascension Flymph or a Tup's Nymph. Flymphs fished as sunk spinners can be fished with many of the same techniques used to fish flymphs as emergers.

A heavy rainbow trout caught on a #16 Pheasant Tail Soft Hackle.

Green Drakes are some of the largest mayflies, averaging a size 10, long-shank hook. *Ephemera guttulata* is the eastern species and *Drunella grandis* is found on western streams. The nymphs are a crawler species, so they are not as available to the fish as swimmer-type mayflies until near the emergence date. At this time, the nymphs migrate to ready themselves for the ascension and the metamorphosis into the adult mayfly. This is the ideal time to fish a nymph. The fish are keying in on these nymphs as their size provides a large meal. Nymphs will produce best as the hatch begins from the bottom to under the surface film and for days after as well. Fishing an Allen's Drake nymph at the proper level is a good choice for imitation when you find yourself on-stream near these emergence periods.

TRICHOPTERA: *Caddisflies*

Caddisflies are of the order Trichoptera and have what is called a complete life cycle. Completing one full generation every year they begin as an egg then hatch into larvae either free drifting or encased and attached to stream rocks. Then they pupa. The pupe continues to live under water. until mature which usually takes about three weeks at which time they swim to the surface and transform into the adult. Flymphs can be a very realistic interpretation of the natural pupa with the soft-hackle fibers imitating legs and antennae both of which reach to slightly beyond the back of the natural pupa's body. Caddis-representative flymphs need to have a fuller and buggier body. My number-one choice for the pupa is a Realist Pupa with the color of the turkey biot abdomen and squirrel hair thorax tied to match the natural's. The buggy fur thorax and segmentation of the abdomen turns a fish's feeding response on. Remember that the fur will be a slightly darker shade when wet. Match the natural's shade by dunking a test sample of fur in a cup of water to check the color it achieves when wet. In very clear water, a darker fly is usually more appropriate if you have to decide between a darker one and lighter one. Another highly productive pattern is the Hare's Ear Soft-Hackle. Its attraction is achieved from the buggy look of the hare's mask dubbing and partridge hackle which move seductively in the current bringing the fly to life. Other caddisfly pupe flymphs include the Emerald Caddis, Red Hackle, Pheasant Tail SHN, Q-Back Flymph, and the Red Possum. The flymphs should be cast downstream and swung with or without line manipulation to achieve an ascending action resembling a caddis pupa swimming to the surface.

Even though you may see many adult caddis on the water or in the air the adult is usually not a target for the fish the reason being that as soon as caddis pupae reach the surface they shed their pupal shell and fly away as adults almost instantly. They don't have to vulnerably ride the currents like mayflies do to dry their wings before they can fly. The trout have an opportunity to consume them as larvae, pupae, and the females again as ovipositing adults. When the female caddis return to the water to lay eggs they do so in various ways. By walking or diving under water. the females cement their eggs to rocks or stream vegetation. Diving female caddis can be under water. for up to 30 minutes laying eggs by breathing with air bubbles trapped between the hair fibers when they dove into the water. The "physical gill" of air bubbles allows the transfer of the carbon dioxide it contains to be diffused in to the water and dissolved oxygen in the water can also be diffused back into the "physical gill". Caddis egg-laying behavior varies between species. *Hydropsyche* species make a diving run under water. then swim to the bottom to lay their eggs. After they lay their eggs, the caddisfly will swim back to the surface where they drift or sometimes fly away again. Fish under these circumstances have many opportunities to eat *Hydropsyche* egg-laying adults. *Brachycentrus* ovipositing adults, otherwise known as Grannoms, will simply drift along riding the currents depositing eggs. A flymph fished like a spent caddis imitates them well. Still other caddis species skitter along the surface or bob up and down on the water over and over again to deposit their eggs. Study and determine the important caddis species found on the river you are fishing. Then match the female's egg-laying behavior accordingly. Something to keep

Red Possum.

in mind about the egg-laying caddis is that the females do this one at a time not in large groups. This egg-laying behavior is not so obvious and you might have to look closely at the stream to determine that it's happening. Often you might see large swarms of caddisflies flying up or down the river. These are hopeful males in search of receptive females for mating. These males are by and large not available to the fish and shouldn't be considered for potential trout-food imitation. But when you do find ovipositing females there is one fly that can imitate all of the egg-laying methods. That fly is a Hare's Ear Soft-Hackle tied with a brown partridge wing covert feather. Use the appropriate colored hare's fur, even dyed fur, to match the color of the body. This flymph can be fished under water. as a diving caddis or it can be fished on top as a spent-wing ovipositing adult. The particular partridge feather used looks very much like a spent caddis wing splayed out on the water. These wing feathers have a mottled pattern that is different than the body feathers and makes them ideal for simulating spent caddis wings.

A Bird's Nest is another very effective pattern for imitating diving egg-laying caddis females. A great technique is to

treat the Bird's Nest with a dry fly powder such as Frog's Fanny dry-fly floatant. This will cause the fly to retain air bubbles as it enters the water, creating an effect similar to the naturals as they dive under water. When fishing a Hare's Ear Soft-Hackle on the surface as a spent egg-laying caddis it should be un-weighted to aid in flotation. When fishing a Hare's Ear Soft-Hackle or Bird's Nest as a diving caddis they should be either un-weighted and fished with a split shot or tied weighted with light-gauge lead to help them break the surface and stay under water.

For surface spent caddis imitation an appropriately shaded Hare's Ear Soft-Hackle should be fished in the film using dry-fly presentation methods. A good strategy for fishing upstream or across stream to the trout is to use a slack-line cast in combination with a 12' Harvey dry-fly leader. You'll want to extend the tippet section until you get plenty of s-curves up to the fly so as to allow for a long, natural drift.

Many western rivers host a large caddisfly known as the October caddis. This Trichoptera is an inch long and is best imitated with pupae and egg-laying patterns. A Red Possum flymph provides a pattern to imitate both the pupae and the egg-laying adult. Fish the pupae with presentations that allow for the fly to rise to the surface in front of a working fish. The Red Possum can also be fished in or under the surface as an egg-laying spent adult. Another good fly for imitating the October caddis pupae is a Red Fox Squirrel-Hair Nymph.

It's important to keep something in mind when matching caddis species. Often we tend to match the length of a caddis natural's head to the back of its wing when choosing an artificial fly hook size. Doing this makes the body length of our artificial too long. If you look at a natural adult caddis from underneath you will see that their body is only .5" to .75" the length of their wings. It's important to match the artificial fly's hook shank to the length of the natural caddis body. This usually means using a hook that is one size smaller than what the adult appears to be at first glance. Always sample the naturals and check their body length when choosing your fly size. For instance in April on my local river the American grannom hatches. This fly appears to be matched with a #18 pupae or adult egg-laying pattern. However, a #18 hook is too long for these caddis bodies and they require a #20 hook to match them correctly. On pupae I tie the soft-hackle collar just slightly longer than the hook shank but on egg-laying adults I tie the soft-hackle collar representing the wings about a hook gape longer than the hook shank for a correctly proportioned interpretation. Match the local Trichoptera as you find them.

Here is a list showing size and body colors for the pupe and adult of the most common trout-stream caddis species.

SPECIES	PUPE COLOR	ADULT COLOR	HOOK SIZE
Hydropsyche (net spinner)	tan or brownish yellow	tan or pale olive	12-16
Brachycentrus (grannom)	olive, charcoal gray	olive, charcoal gray	14-20
Oecetis (longhorn sedge)	reddish brown	golden or green	16-18
Dicosmoecus (October caddis)	orange	orange	6
Chimarra (little black sedge)	black	black	18-20
Agraylea (micro caddis)	dark gray	dark gray	20-24
Lepidostoma (little brown sedge)	brownish olive	brownish olive	18

DIPTERA: *Midge*

Chironomid or midge species are probably the smallest flies you will ever have to imitate. These are flies of the order Diptera and are very common and widespread. On my local water these flies hatch year round and are an important source of food for the trout. Some of the best fishing is during the winter when midges along with blue-winged olives provide the most predictable surface action of the year. Midge can be very small with sizes #18-#28 being common. In fact on this particular river the average size is a #26, and the fish know it. The trout can be very selective to the size, shape, color, and behavior of these naturals.

Midge larvae are available to the fish everyday, but it's during the pupal stage that the surface activity starts. The reason that the fish key in on the pupal stage is that being so small these flies have a hard time breaking through the surface tension of the water. It takes them a little while to break through the surface but when they do they fly away almost instantly so the trout key in on the pupae as an efficient target. Midge pupae hang vertically just under the surface as they drift downstream trying to break through the water surface and the distance they drift before breaking through the surface can be considerable. This is the most vulnerable stage in the lifecycle of the midge and gives the trout plenty of opportunity for an easy meal. The pupae come in many colors gray, olive, black, red, brown, cream. However I feel that the matching the correct size is crucial, followed by color is most important in imitating these insect lifeforms. When the pupae are two

Pheasant Tail Soft Hackle.

Brassie Flymph.

millimeters long and drifting in water currents, color alone isn't the most important factor. Size, shape, and presentation count for more. I've tried all sorts of midge pupa patterns, made with foam, CDC, glass beads, etc., but it wasn't until I adapted a flymph to imitate midges that I knew I had found a most consistently effective pupa imitation. My go-to pattern is a small Pheasant Tail Soft-Hackle without a tail for midging trout. I tie this pattern down to a size 28 and it performs wonderfully with proper presentations. Another pattern that works to imitate the pupa effectively is the Brassie Flymph. A variation of the common Brassie, with the added attraction of the soft-hackle collar, it's tied using fine wire in the desired color to match the natural pupae. I use a 12' Harvey style leader with either a 6X or 7X extended tippet section. If you want to keep the flymph from sinking too deep, apply fly floatant to the tippet up to about 1.5" from the fly. This will allow the fly to drift, depending on the presentation, in or just under the surface film where the pupae are. I feel the success of this pattern is due to the soft-hackle feather fibers. On a fly this small, the soft-hackle fibers are hardly noticeable when wet, but can be the trigger

in getting a fish to strike as they imitate movement and life. Presentation is of utmost importance when fishing to midging trout.

These situations usually take place in slow-moving, flat-water environments and the fish get a good long look at these flies. I use either a slack-line cast with a reach mend or if I want the fly to have a little movement I will use a down-and-across swing cast. Fish it down and across dead drift or with short tugs or line stripping during the drift. Making short, relatively quick strips of line as the fly approaches in front of the fish is often important in slow- moving water situations, such as pools and flats, because this activates the soft-hackle fibers making the fly come to life. A series of line strips of about an inch each are all that is necessary to make the fly "swim". When the fish takes the fly, use the slip strike to avoid pulling the hook out. To keep the hook-set play the fish very lightly, especially after the initial strike, as these hooks are so small they need to be set in the jaw or mouth firmly to avoid coming loose.

On a recent trip I fished a small, very cold tailwater that had sections where fish were rising to midges the entire day. The

anglers that were catching the largest, most selective fish were doing so only if they could match the size, shape, and color, as well as achieve realistic behavior, with their fly patterns because these fish see thousands of the same natural midge pupae and adults every day of the year. A #24 Pheasant Tail Soft-Hackle combined with a 12' 7X leader and presented with a Hidy subsurface swing with a series of short line strips through the slow-moving water was effective in taking many of these brown and rainbow trout. Midges are important insects and many rivers have trout that count on them for a large part of their diet. Chironomids have a longer hatch season than any other trout stream aquatic insect providing surface activity on many rivers 12 months of the year. They are often overlooked by fishermen, but not by the fish. Once you learn the complexities of catching fish during a midge hatch you can consider yourself a true "far and fine" angler.

AMPHIPODA: *Crustacean*

An aquatic trout food that is very important and often overlooked by fishermen in fertile spring creeks or tailwaters is the freshwater crustacean. The freshwater crustacean or scud is found in many spring-creek-type environments and often can be the most prolific source of trout food. The fish in these fertile streams depend on scuds for a majority of their diet because the scud is very nutritious containing a large caloric intake per individual. Streams with healthy populations of these crustaceans are home to trout that can reach some very heavy weights. A scud is not an insect, but rather a crustacean from the order Amphipoda.

One reason that they are disregarded is that ordinarily fishermen never see them. They spend their entire lives underwater, unlike most trout stream aquatic insects which will be seen on the surface or in the air during a hatch at least some time during the year. A wet-fly can be tied to imitate scuds; a good fly to carry if you fish spring creeks or tailwaters is the Scud Soft-Hackle. The color of this artificial should match the naturals in your local water. The most common colors are usually a shade or mixture of gray, olive, tan, black, cream, orange, and pink. You need to sample your stream to match the shade found, but if you aren't able to do this tan or olive seem to be the most common shades. When pregnant the female scud displays an orange egg sack in the rear part of her translucent body. If desired, tie this pattern with the correct color fur for the body and orange fur near the bend of the hook to imitate a pregnant scud.

Scuds are found in slow-moving sections of streams living within the abundant aquatic vegetation, such as elodea or potamogeton, but also swimming freely throughout the stream bottom. They are less concentrated in silted areas or in faster currents. Sunlight has an effect on the behavior of scuds. They are more active during periods of low light. Sunrise and sunset along with cloudy, overcast days are better for imitating an active swimming scud coming out of the vegetation to move around. These creatures swim with a straightened body profile, so using a straight-shank hook is more natural for imitating a swimming scud whereas the resting or hanging crustaceans have a more curved profile and are better imitated with curved hooks. Tie the scud with very sparse hackle as the fibers are not meant to imitate emerging wings like on the mayfly and caddisfly flymphs, but rather to imitate the crustacean's legs, tail, antennae and movement in general. Trim the top hackle collar fibers and finish the head by pulling the remaining fibers underneath the hook. It's important to weight the

Scud Soft Hackle.

hook only on the front half of the hook shank and flatten the lead, so the fly will drift right-side up. The legs on the naturals are constantly circulating water over the gills and soft-hackle fibers offer a good imitation of this movement.

The swimming motion of scuds is a swim-and-pause movement with streaks of 6"-10" and then a pause to rest and breathe. They are very good swimmers, so fishing the artificial with an intermittent rod-tip twitch can look natural while other times you need a slow dead-drift presentation. A series of short line strips, as the fly is across and downstream of the angler, of about 6" followed by a pause also works well as it pulls the fly off the bottom for a moment and

then allows the fly to drop down again, similar to the actual scud swimming motion. I like to use the 8'11" nymph leader for this fly with split shot in combination with a weighted scud. Using a flymph mending swing, cast up and across stream to allow the fly to sink to the bottom for a good deep drift. You need to fish these flies close to the bottom as they spend their entire life there. Use hump mends to keep the artificial drifting on the bottom naturally with a little rod-tip action every now and then through the drift to simulate the swim-and-pause movement. When the fly begins to swing make a hump mend releasing a little line into the drift to slow its swing down. You don't want the fly to rise to the surface as with other wet-fly swings. At other times you need to use a drag-free presentation allowing the scud to drift without any imparted manipulation. For dead drifting a scud use a tuck cast and high stick nymphing tactics up and across stream. Follow the fly through the drift lowering the rod tip and keeping it slightly in front of the fly to keep the line and the soft-hackled wet-fly from dragging.

Scuds are found in and among sub-surface weed beds such as the elodea shown here.

Scuds vary in size, and they grow bigger through their life span, ranging in size from #10-#18 in most spring creeks. The two most common species are the *Gammarus* and the *Hyalella*. The *Gammarus* is the larger of the two species, however the *Hyalella* is found in more types of spring creeks. The *Gammarus* is limited to streams that have high levels of dissolved calcium in the water compostition as the species needs high levels of this mineral to form it's exoskeleton. *Gammarus* range from size #10 to #18 while the *Hyalella* are #18 or #20.

You can inspect the color and size of the naturals on a stream by searching through a handful of aquatic vegetation where they cling. Match the color and size of your artificial to the appearance of the scuds you find in the water. This is a good time to have a portable fly-tying kit at streamside. Carry rabbit fur dubbing in assorted scud colors to help you imitate the local bugs specifically. Be sure to weight the hook to some degree as these flies need to be on the bottom or close to the bottom at all times. If you get to a spring creek and find scuds in the stream sample, a Scud Soft-Hackle might be the only fly you have to fish all day long to catch fish.

PLECOPTERA: *Stoneflies*

The largest aquatic insects you will ever need to imitate are the stoneflies. These insects are of the order Plecotpera, and the largest species found in North America is *Pteronarcys californica*, otherwise known as the salmonfly. In many western waters these stonefly nymphs are 2.5 inchs long and are a staple in the diet of large trout. When the adults begin to hatch in early summer, the trout rivers of the West attract many anglers wishing to catch the large trout that key in on the nymphs. Stonefly nymphs are the most available life stage of the insect to the fish. The nymphs begin to crawl out of the water after three years of maturing in the stream. During this emergence the nymphs will crawl up on rocks, logs, or shore structure to hatch into the winged adult. Many large nymphs will be dislodged during the emergence and drift helplessly in the current making themselves available to the trout.

Stoneflies prefer fast, well-oxygenated stream sections such as riffles. The largest emergences occur in the morning and evening making them the best times to find the fish tuned-in to the hatch.

Stoneflies take up to an hour to fully free themselves from their nymphal shucks and the low-light conditions offer protection for them, making them less susceptible to predators like birds. These insects are available to the fish year-round, crawling amid rocks on the stream bottom so they can be fished at any time, however in the early spring about two weeks before the adults hatch and again in the fall are the peak periods for the nymph's attention. While some adults are available to the fish when they get blown into the currents, the nymphs are the primary target since the adults emerge on structure above the water. The PT Stone Soft-Hackle was designed to imitate *Pteronarcys californica* specifically, but the squirrel body fur color and size can be altered to imitate the stoneflies you find locally. The soft-hackle collar on this fly imitates the moving legs of the natural looking for a foothold among the stream rocks. The natural nymphs don't swim well and if they are dislodged from structure they will tumble until they can find a foothold again. Fish this soft-hackled nymph with a drag-free drift on the bottom of the stream.

The PT Stone Soft-Hackle is a heavily weighted fly and gives new meaning to term "sinks like a stone (fly)". This wet-fly can be fished with only a lead underbody and bead for the weight or can be used in conjunction with the needed amount of split shot on the leader. The split shot will also slow down the stonefly nymph's drift in fast currents allowing for a more natural drift. Since the weight on the hook shank causes the hook to ride upside down with the point up, the front of the shank should be bent with an upward angle. When the fly is flipped over this will give the pattern a natural look of movement.

Casting all this weight calls for a slower casting stroke, a more open loop and a stout leader. I like to use the 8' 11" nymph leader with a 3X tippet. The tuck cast can still be used, but must be slowed down so you don't get a tailing loop. Allow the line to straighten behind you on the backcast then make a smooth transition gradually applying power to the forward cast before checking the rod and making the wrist snap. Keep the line, leader, and wet-fly under control. As the fly drifts on the bottom follow the fly with your rod tip looking for any sign of a fish striking the fly. Maintain the line

Pt Stone Soft Hackle.

Stoneflies require a well-oxygenated environment such as this riffle water.

and leader relatively tight so you can detect strikes, but slack enough to allow a natural drift. This is a balance of line control and leader weight distribution. If the wet-fly is drifting too fast add weight to the leader, if it's getting hung up too much take weight off the leader. However make sure you are fishing on the bottom. You're deep enough when your fly is catching vegetation or rocks every now and then because that's were stoneflies live. Be sure to clean the hook of any vegetation between casts. With a fly this big and heavy you should be able to feel the fly tumbling over the rocks through the fly rod. Strikes when dead-drifting the PT Stone Soft-Hackle can be either strong or subtle so be ready and set the hook when necessary.

READING THE WATER AND FINDING FISH

Being able to read the trout stream is vital to locating fish and having your presentations mean something. You might not be able to see the trout but if you can look at the water and get the feeling that a trout is lying in a certain location you're going to stand a better chance of catching fish more consistently. There are many water characteristics that will allow you to get a good idea of where fish could be holding. They can really be broken down into two main categories: above-stream structure characteristics and below-stream structure characteristics. When you are looking at the water the easiest clues are the ones most obvious above the water. Structure such as large rocks, tree trunks or limbs that are down in the water enough to slow the current and provide a resting place for a fish are good locations to target. Look for the slack water or eddy's they create. The slack water can be both in front of and behind the object. The water will travel faster on the sides of the structure and food items will be channeled through here. Fish will hold in the slack water in front of or in back of the structure and grab food as it passes by through the faster water channels. Eddy's are reverse current slack water areas behind structure. It's energy efficient for fish to hold here as food items get caught in the current, accumulating and allowing an easy meal for the fish. The eddy's water can build up food especially on the surface. A good strategy is to try presentations into both the faster side channels and then into the eddy's. You will need to mend to slow down the fly's drift in both of these places to allow the fish an opportunity to strike.

Below-stream structures cause the same

hydraulic effects except that they will be more subtle in appearance to the angler. Begin by utilizing your polarized sunglasses to look for under water. structure. The sunglasses will cut the light reflecting off the water and allow you to see into the water much more clearly. To find the fish's holding lies first look for the obvious, the fish. If the water is clear enough and not too broken you will be surprised at how many times you can spot fish if you take the time and really look for them. Vince Marinaro, when talking about spotting fish, said that, 'you have to convince yourself that if there are fish in the water you will see them'.

When spotting fish sub-surface it often means looking for tail or body movements. However under slower water conditions you might see the fish move or you might not. In this case also look for a body outline which can be well camouflaged against the stream bottom. If the water is fast or broken and spotting a fish is more difficult look for the same objects that appear above stream. Rocks, boulders, tree limbs or any solid object that displaces water will be a potential holding location for a trout. These objects might only be seen as darker or lighter areas in relation to other features on the stream bottom, but you need to learn to recognize sub-surface structure the same as you would above-stream structure. This comes with observation and experience. It's important to understand the relationship between under water. structure and feeding or sheltering lies.

Fish, especially large ones, hold in areas that provide food, protection, and efficient expenditure of energy, the same needs that humans and other animals have. The prime lies meet all of these criteria. A lie that has abundant food drifting through, sufficient dissolved oxygen levels, as well as offering protection in the form of structure, be it tree trunks, weeds, or undercut banks, will hold fish. Remember though that these lies must be energy efficient. Trout use more energy in moving water than in still water as they hold in the current and a slower current lie requires less energy than a faster one. So a fish might give up a lie that has large amounts of food channeled into it in favor of a lie that offers a little less food, but better energy-expenditure-to-food ratio.

There are ways to read the water and find fish by only looking at the current. The water currents physical features are a direct result of the cfs (cubic feet per second), the depth, and the stream-bottom structure. Fast, shallow water over boulders or rocks will be seen as riffles. Slower, deeper water over gravel, sand, silt or vegetation will be seen as glassy and flat, almost still. Between these two extremes are many current conditions. The idea is to use the current to give you an idea of where fish might be holding. Runs can be fished by targeting the current seams between the faster and slower water. Look for velocity changes which indicate the change between the two current speeds. Sometimes these velocity changes are all a fish needs for a feeding lie. The trout will hold in the slower current seam right next to the faster water and as food drifts by in the faster water the fish will grab it then move back into the slower, more energy-efficient current. Cast the soft-hackle nymph above the fish into the fast water on the edge of the slow-water seam. Trout hold in the slower water next to faster water to intercept food items passing by. Present the fly on the edge of the faster water not in the middle of the slower water. Use the current seams to target your presentations. The trout won't move far to take the fly in the faster water, so you really need to target the potential fish and place the fly well.

The classic riffle, run, pool stream characteristic is a good example of how currents influence food distribution. As the riffle slows into the run much food is dislodged from the riffle section by the fast water. These insects are disrupted from rocks or while trying to emerge are swept downstream by the current. The head of the run below a riffle makes a fine place for a feeding lie because so much food is coming down to the fish and the water is not as fast, making it more efficient to intercept the drifting food items. Similarly the tail of a pool is a good location for targeting fish because this where any food that has drifted down from the upstream riffle and run are going to be channeled. The water at the tail is usually comfortable for the fish to hold in and food items come to the trout. Trout have a pecking order that is fairly predictable. Most of the time you will find the largest fish in the tail of the pool while the smaller fish will be found in the middle or at the head of the pool. Larger fish can be found at the head of the pool, but the largest fish are usually holding in the tai. Keep this in mind when you position yourself to cast. The reason

for this pecking order reflects the characteristics of food drift and water speed. By holding in the back of the pool the largest trout has the most prime feeding lie conditions. The water is slow enough to be energy efficient while the food from the riffle and pool above his location is channeled into him providing the most amount of food with the least amount of energy expenditure. While the pecking order in a pool is that the large fish is usually at the tail of the pool, open-water runs or riffles are less predictable. However, the largest fish will always occupy the choicest lies that offer the largest food drift, most efficient current speed, and protection as well.

Spring creeks that have less visible water structure characteristics can be a greater challenge in locating fish. The fish in these streams often use the abundant aquatic vegetation as their holding and feeding lies. As the season progresses the vegetation grows and begins to choke the

stream. The fish then use the open channels between the plants as shelter. The water velocity is usually rather uniform in these low-gradient spring creeks and fish can be found about anywhere there is an open channel offering food and shelter. A good approach is to first try to visually spot a fish. Working from the bank and staying low, get into position to make the cast. Remember to strive for "invisibility" from the fish. In faster spring creek or broken water conditions, use 'reading the water' techniques to locate potential fish.

Fishing sub-surface is often challenging in spring creeks because of the aquatic vegetation which quite often reaches to the surface of the stream. To make it easier target your fish and make shorter drifts through the water to keep the fly from picking up vegetation. Check the fly often and keep it free from any vegetation. More important than all of the criteria we have discussed above for

The holding water that rocks create results in pockets and seams that are easy to distinguish.

locating trout is a trout stream's dissolved-oxygen content followed closely by water temperature. As discussed earlier, trout need to have cold, clean water and good dissolved oxygen levels to survive. Trout can survive for a short period of time at the upper temperature extremes if the water has enough oxygen for them to maintain a healthy physiology. But this at the extreme and overall trout still need cold water as a basic necessity and will be found where the water temperature is most conducive to body function. To help you locate these areas, take the water temperature and use this to gauge stream locations that will offer the best fishing opportunities. A trout stream's very existence is dependent on the temperature of the water it holds. Water temperature not only affects the trout's metabolism, but also their need for oxygen.

Dissolved oxygen (DO) molecules are located between the water molecules and are measured in parts per million (ppm). Dissolved oxygen in quality trout streams is considered to be 8 to 10 ppm. Colder water can hold more DO because the water molecules, as well as the oxygen molecules, are moving slowly which allows there to be a tighter consolidation of the oxygen molecules in between the water molecules. As the water temperature increases, the water molecules begin moving faster and colliding with the dissolved oxygen molecules which in turn spread the DO molecules out, even pushing them out of the water entirely. At lower water temperatures from 40^0 to 50^0 even though the water is saturated with DO, the cold water slows down the fish's metabolism so their need for food is decreased and they may become lethargic. The best technique for sub-surface fishing in colder water temperatures is a slow, deeply drifted soft-hackled nymph. Try getting the fly right in front of the fish because they will not move far under these conditions.

As the water temperatures increase into the middle 50's the food chain begins to be more active. Ideal water temperatures for trout and the food base are between 55^0-65^0. Between these temperatures the stream is at its most active. The fish metabolism is up and they are looking for food.

Also their food base is more active.

Riffles are fertile food areas with high oxygen levels.

The Hidy Subsurface Swing is an effective approach in targeting a spotted fish.

Learn to spot fish in the water by their shape and movement.

By late summer a spring creeks vegetation has reached its largest amount. These plants are superior oxygenators during photosynthesis but respire when the sun is down. In late season with heavy vegetation it's wise to wait until after sunrise to fish. That way you give the plants time to recover the dissolved oxygen levels.

From zooplankton to nymphs to the forage fish like sculpins the whole ecosystem is in full swing. The trout's metabolism is also increasing and they are feeding more. The fishing will continue to be good until the water temperature reaches about 68°. At this point the water begins to hold less oxygen gases between the water molecules. Even though the insect life is still active, the warmer water begins to slow the fish's metabolism and his feeding patterns as well. If the water temperatures continue to increase into the 70's the trout begin to face stressful conditions. Prolonged periods of upper 70's can be fatal unless oxygen levels are sufficiently high from aeration through stream turbulence. At these higher water temperatures the oxygen levels are low and the fish is using the oxygen as fast as it takes it in. The trout's metabolism changes and its need for food lessens while internally it tries to adapt to take in more oxygen and lower its body temperature. In these cases, look for any springs or feeder streams where water temperatures would be regulated to lower levels. The fish will actively seek out the locations that are the most comfortable. When water temperatures are high the fish will congregate where the water has more oxygen introduced by aeration. Such places are at the base of water falls or pocket-water where the rocks and riffles churn the water adding dissolved oxygen.

If the water is above 72° it's best to leave the fish alone until the water is a more suitable temperature. One way to find lower water temperatures is to fish when the water has had time to cool off from thermal heating, such as in the early morning before sunrise. At night, the lack of thermal daytime heating allows the stream temperatures to fall. The lowest water temperatures are just before sunrise and so early morning fishing is most productive during periods of increased water temperatures. Remember however that on spring creeks with vast amounts of aquatic vegetation, dissolved oxygen levels drop at night and are lowest just before sunrise, increasing throughout the daytime hours, so wait until the after the sun comes up to fish under these conditions. On spring creeks the water temperature remains fairly consistent with spring sources of 50°-57° year round, so thermal heating during the daytime hours is not as much of an issue. A stream thermometer will help you understand the importance

Underwater springs provide stable water temperatures.

of thermal conditions and also allows you to become a more knowledgeable angler regarding trout feeding and holding locations. To summarize you will find trout where these criteria are met in order of importance:

1 PROTECTION FROM PREDATORS—Fish need shelter and this can be found under overhanging stream banks, behind or in front of in-stream rocks, submerged trees, and between or under aquatic weed beds. This is the most important basic survival requirement for obvious reasons – to keep from being eaten.

2 SUFFICIENT DISSOLVED OXYGEN LEVELS— Trout will relocate to find higher oxygen levels if necessary. This is the most important environmental characteristic they seek. Fish can survive at the upper temperature limits for a short period of time if the DO levels are sufficient.

3 WATER TEMPERATURE—Trout and the food base are most active between 55°-65°. A trout's metabolism and physiology are most efficient within this range and the trout will be more likely to be actively feeding.

4 FOOD SUPPLY—Trout will lie in locations that provide for the highest caloric intake with the least amount of energy expenditure. While eating is obviously important, the other criteria rank higher among immediate basic needs. For while the trout can go a couple of weeks without eating if forced to, these

other needs are imperative every second of every day. Look for trout in locations that allow conservation of energy, yet have good food supply channels.

In review, trout will be found where the most conducive conditions exist for their comfort and safety, and the largest fish will be found where conditions are not only met but most ideal. Trout, as you can see, live in the middle of a finely balanced ecosystem that the complete angler must understand.

PUTTING IT ALL TOGETHER

When you get to the stream, before even tying on a fly, you need to first read the water and answer the questions of fish location, what may be hatching, and which fly you will use to imitate the hatch or if there is no hatch which fly you will fish and the depth you will fish it. After these questions have been answered and a wet-fly selected you should choose the most appropriate leader that will allow you to present the fly in the most effective manner. If you are fishing a flymph you should decide the depth under the surface you want the fly to be, if any, and in answer to that question whether or not you need to use floatant on the leader to suspend the fly at the correct depth. On the other hand if you are going to be fishing deep with soft-hackled nymphs ask yourself if you need to use split shot, a weighted or un-weighted wet-fly, or a two-fly dropper leader. This depends on the water depth and current speed. Taking a stream insect sample is very beneficial in

helping you identify the insect and just as important the stage of the insect that the trout are keying in on. If you haven't fished the water before or even if you have, it's necessary to take a stream sample. There are a few stream sample methods that are helpful. The first is a surface sample that collects bugs from the surface down to about a foot below the surface. This sample is conducted using a small seine screen of about 14" x 10". Stretch the net out and take a sample of a current section that has the best chance of containing a representative drift of insects. If the fish are rising and you want to look at the bugs that are drifting over them, position yourself at a safe distance upstream or downstream of the exact line of drift and take a surface sample. When you collect the bugs in the seine you may find more than one species of insect. Oftentimes on fertile streams there are multiple insect species hatching at the same time. When this is happening and there are many life stages of these insects occurring at the same time, this is called a "complex hatch".

The trout are going to key in on one of these species and possibly one of its life stages (nymph, emerger, adult, egg-layer). You need to decipher the correct one quickly. Hatches can last minutes to hours but the sooner you can adapt to the selective fish's appetite the better your chances will be of taking fish.

If you find only two species of insects hatching at once then this called a "compound hatch".

Inspect the seine sample closely. You

Trout move to higher oxygenated water if stream temperatures increase.

Notice the slack current pocket downstream behind the log. This is a prime lie because the fish has the luxury of intercepting food items that drift by the current seam as well as having the safety of the structure. A Flymph Mending Swing allows the fly to drift along the edge of the current seam before swinging across stream.

may find there is a larger #16 PMD dun or two, as well as smaller #20 grannom caddis pupae and adults. The caddis however may greatly outnumber the mayflies. In this case if you're just watching the water and air the larger more visible PMD's are hiding the presence of the smaller grannoms. This is called a "masking hatch". This situation can particularly be true of caddis, as they may not be visible on the surface yet the fish are feeding heavily underneath the surface on the pupae. Another time is when there may be a hatch of #18 pale morning duns and smaller #22 Baetis mayflies coming off at the same time. The larger PMD's are quite visible yet they are distracting the attention away from the fact that what the fish are actually feeding on is the smaller, darker Baetis.

In addition to the seine sampling, watch individual adults on the water to see if they are being eaten. If the fish are taking adults you will be able to observe this, however it could be that the fish are keying in on the emergers or pupae. This is why sampling the water with a seine is so important. It gives you the information you need to know most about the insect species that are hatching. After you have determined the target species and its size

and color you can then start presenting the fish with emergers or adult patterns for that species. Remember that trout will often feed on the species hatching in the greatest numbers, regardless of size, and frequently this means a smaller caddis, mayfly, or midge species during a complex or compound hatch. During a masking hatch, if a highly visible mayfly like a PMD floats over a rising fish without a rise and a second later the fish rises to what looks like a smaller Baetis, then first try a smaller, darker flymph. However, it could be that the fish is indeed taking PMD's, but is keying in on the sub-surface or surface film nymphs and emergers. That is the beauty of the flymph. You will always be imitating the emerger with them, which is usually the correct stage to imitate during a hatch, and you simply need to pick the right size and color and then make a quality presentation.

Another intricacy to a compound hatch is the "mimicking hatch". This is a situation where two flies of the same color, but not of the same size, are hatching. For instance, perhaps size 18 Baetis are highly visible in the air and on the water, but in reality the fish are keying in on smaller size 24 *Pseudocloeons*. Both of these mayflies are blue-winged olives, but are

greatly different in size. In this case the fish are seeing more of the smaller *Pseudocloeons* and this is providing them with more food to eat overall even though the individual flies are smaller. The only way you can know this is to be observant. It helps to become a trout for a moment in your mind's eye and to think like they would concerning the food that is available. Trout may think, "I'm going to choose a particular food item and stick with it for a while. I'm going to choose the particular fly species with the greatest numbers floating in front of me or I'm going to pick micro-caddis even though the little olive mayflies look good." By rolling these kinds of ideas around in your head you remove yourself from the predator's point of view and for a moment take on your prey's point of view which you must understand in order to catch the prey.

Watching individual fish and observing their rise forms can also give you some further information as to which species and life stage the fish are feeding on. For instance, a splashy rise is often indicative of a trout that is chasing emergers, such as caddis pupae as they swim to the stream surface. On the other hand, a rise ring of a fish that is feeding on emerging mayflies will usually be very delicate because the fish is "sipping" the vulnerable emergers that are drifting in or just under the surface film and the trout is not completely breaking through the surface with their mouths. A dorsal and tail fin rise can also indicate emerger activity as the fish "rolls" on the emergers. Trout can actually cause a surface disturbance that visually looks similar to a rise by flicking their tail while holding up to a foot under the surface. This is an indication that the fish is feeding on sub-surface nymphs. To illicit a strike from such a fish, try swinging a soft-hackled nymph at the appropriate depth, allowing the fly to rise toward the surface in front of the fish. Another rise form is that of a trout feeding on adult mayfly duns, adult caddis, or large terrestrials on top of the surface. This fish will often display its mouth or head above water or have a rise ring with air bubbles left behind from the fish's gills expelling air as they suck in the fly. And finally, a fish feeding on mayfly spinners, spent caddis, midge pupae, or small terrestrials like ants often exhibit a rise form that is quite subtle with the fish leisurely sucking in these low surface-riding insects.

It's in moments like this that fly fishing's innate beauty is fully realized. Fishing for large trout rising to midges is not only technically challenging but it's also exciting. You can match local midge species with a Midge Soft Hackle in the appropriate thread body color.

Vince Marinaro observed that highly selective trout will often drift many feet downstream, while still facing upstream, carefully studying a food item in the surface film in order to determine its authenticity before rising to consume it. These fish then return upstream to the feeding station where they started. Under these circumstances an angler needs to be aware that the fish is actually holding upstream a number of feet from where their rise is observed and should cast and present the fly accordingly. After you have analyzed all of these stream conditions choose an appropriate imitation, get into casting position, and make a presentation that will most likely result in the flymph looking like a natural with similar behavior. Observance is the name of the game and is what makes trout fly-fishing so special, it is a thinking man's sport.

The second stream sample method is a stream-bottom kick sample. For this you need a larger seine screen about 2' x 2'. Place the seine screen in the water at a 90-degree angle to the bottom. Hold the screen so that any drifting insect will be caught while drifting downstream. You may want to stir up and dislodge some nymphs from the rocks or vegetation just upstream of the net with your foot. Take care not to tear up the bottom structure. This stream sample method will show the nymphs and larvae found in the stream and allow you to choose a soft-hackled nymph to best imitate the size, shape, color, and behavior of the naturals. If you don't have a seine screen you can pick up and examine stream rocks, pick through aquatic vegetation, or watch the surface just upstream of your wading position to see if you can get a visual determination of the hatch. If there is no hatch and you want to choose a sub-surface wet-fly, either choose based on the time of year and the insects that may be active or simply pick the fly that best represents the largest and most common biomass in the stream you are fishing.

After you have located stream conditions most favorable to hold feeding fish, chosen the fly, tied on the leader and fly, and positioned yourself for the cast, then it's time to make the cast to a suspected or known fish. Have confidence in your fly, choice of casting location, presentation, and tackle. If you are confident that you have made the best choices, your fishing success will reflect this.

Soft-hackled nymphs and flymphs are very good fish motivators. The traditional patterns are still very effective and the modern flies will allow you to imitate scuds, stoneflies, smaller caddis, mayflies, and midges. The longer I fish shn's and flymphs the more I am impressed by their lifelike ability to attract fish. They can take you beyond merely formulaic fishing out into the open trout streams of unlimited presentation choices. Perhaps most importantly they are just incredibly exciting to fish with. So get out there, catch some trout and have fun.

HERE IS A LIST OF SUPPLIERS FOR MATERIALS:

- **English Angling Trappings at Angler's Den**
  11 East Main Street,
  Pawling, NY 12564
  Tel. 845-855-5182
  http://www.anglers-den.com

- **National Feather-Craft Feather-Craft Fly Fishing**
  8307 Manchester Rd. St. Louis,
  MO 63144
  Tel. 800-659-1707
  www.feather-craft.com

- **Cookshill Fly Tying Materials**
  M Holding, Roughcote Lane,
  Caverswall, Stoke-on-Trent,
  Staffordshire, ST11 9ES UK
  Tel. +44 1782 388382
  www.Cookshill-flytying.co.uk

- **Bob Marriott's Fly Fishing**
  2700 W. Orangethorpe Ave. Fullerton,
  CA 92833
  Tel. 800-535-6633
  www.bobmarriotts.com

- **Blue Ribbon Flies**
  305 Canyon St. West Yellowstone,
  MT. 59758
  Tel. 406-646-7642
  www.blueribbonflies.com

- **Madison River Fishing Company**
  109 Main Street Box 627 Ennis,
  MT 59729
  Tel. 800-227-7127
  www.mrfc.com

BIBLIOGRAPHY

- Bergman, Ray.; *Trout*, Penn Publishing, Philadelphia, Pennsylvania, 1938.
- Berner, Dame Juliana.; *The Treatyse of Fysshynge wyth an Angle*, Sopwell, Enlgand, 1497.
- Blacker, William.; *Art of Fly Making*, London, England, 1855.
- Blades, William.; *Fishing Flies and Fly Tying*, Stackpole, Harrisburg, Pennsylvania, 1951.
- Borger, Gary A.; *Presentation*, Tomorrow River Press, Wausau, Wisconsin, 1995.
- Chetham, James.; *The Angler's Vade Mecum*, London, England, 1681.
- Cutcliffe, H. C.; *The Art of Trout Fishing in Rapid Streams*, South Molton, England, 1863.
- Edmonds, Harfield H. and Lee, Norman N.; *Brook and River Trouting*, Bradford, England, 1916.
- Francis, Francis.; *A Book on Angling*; Longmans, Green and Co., London, England, 1867.
- Grove, Alvin.; *The Lure and Lore of Trout Fishing*, Stackpole, Harrisburg, Pennsylvania, 1951.
- Harvey, George W.; *Techniques of Trout Fishing and Fly Tying*, Metz Hatchery, Belleville, Pennsylvania, 1985.
- Harvey, George W. and Shields, Daniel L.; *George Harvey: Memories, Patterns and Tactics*, DLS Enterprises, Lemont, Pennsylvania, 1989.
- Hidy, Vernon S.; *Sports Illustrated Wet-Fly Fishing*, J. B. Lippincott Co., Philadelphia & New York, 1960.
- Hidy, Vernon S.; "The Art of Fishing the Flymph-Part One, the Flymph Phenomenon", *Fly Fisherman Magazine*, St. Louis, Missouri, May, 1971.
- Hidy, Vernon S.; "Fishing the Flymph II the Dry Fly and the Flymph: A Parallel", *Fly Fisherman Magazine*, St. Louis, Missouri, July, 1971.
- Hidy, Vernon S.; *Sports Illustrated Fly Fishing*, J.B. Lippincott, Philadelphia, Pennsylvania, 1972.
- Hidy, Vernon S.; *The Pleasures of Fly Fishing*, Winchester Press, New York, New York, 1972.
- Hidy, Vernon S.; *The Masters on the Nymph*, "Soft-Hackled Nymphs-The Flymphs, Doubleday, New York, New York, 1979.
- Hughes, Dave; *Wet Flies: Tying and Fishing Soft-Hackles*, Stackpole, Harrisburg, Pennsylvania, 1994.
- Humphreys, Joseph B.; *Joe Humphreys's Trout Tactics*, Stackpole, Mechanicsburg, Pennsylvania, 1981.
- Humphreys, Joseph B.; *On The Trout Stream with Joe Humphreys*, Stackpole, Harrisburg, Pennsylvania, 1989.
- Jackson, Hohn.; *The Practical Fly Fisher*, Bradford, England 1853.
- Kirkbridge, John.; *The Northern Anglers*, London, England, 1855.
- Kissane, Joseph A. and Schweitzer Steven B.; *Drag-Free Drift: Leader Design and Presentation Techniques for Fly Fishing*, Stackpole, Mechanicsburg, Pennsylvania, 2001.
- Kite, Oliver.; *Nymph Fishing In Practice*, Herbert Jenkins, London, England, 1963.
- LaFontaine, Gary.; *Caddisflies*, Lyons & Burford, Winchester Press/Nick Lyons, New York, New York, 1981.
- Leisenring, James E.; *The Art of Tying the Wet Fly*, Dodd, Mead and Co., New York, New York, 1941.
- Leisenring, James E. and Hidy, Vernon S.; *The Art of Tying the Wet Fly and Fishing the Flymph*, Crown Publishers, New York, New York, 1971.
- Magee, Leslie.; *Fly Fishing: The North Country Tradition*, Smith Settle, London, England, 1994.
- Nemes, Sylvester.; *The Soft-Hackled Fly*; Chatham Press, Old Greenwich, Connecticut, 1975.
- Nemes, Sylvester.; *The Soft-Hackled Fly Addict*, by the Author, Chicago, Illinois, 1981.
- Nemes, Sylvester.; *Soft-Hackled Fly Imitations*, by the Author, Bozeman, Montana, 1991.
- Nemes, Sylvester.; *Two Centuries of Soft-Hackled Flies: A Survey of the Literature Complete With Original Patterns, 1747-Present*, Stackpole Books, Mechanicsburg, Pennsylvania, 2004.
- Ovington, Ray.; *How to Take Trout on Wet Flies and Nymphs*, Little, Brown & Co., Boston, Massachusetts, 1952.
- Pritt, T.E.; *Yorkshire Trout Flies*; Goodall and Suddick, Leeds, England, 1885.
- Pritt, T.E.; *North Country Flies*, Sampson Low, Marston, Searle, & Rivington, London, England, 1886.
- Pritt, T.E.; *The Book of Grayling*, Goodall and Suddick, Leeds, England, 1888.
- Ronalds, Alfred.; *A Fly Fisher's Entomology*, Longman, Rees, Orme, Brown, Green, and Longman, London, England, 1836.
- Rosborough, E.H. "Polly".; *Tying and Fishing the Fuzzy Nymphs*, by the Author, Chiloquin, Oregon, 1965.
- Sawyer, Frank.; *Keeper of the Stream*; A & C Black, London, England, 1952.
- Sawyer, Frank.; *Nymphs and the Trout*, A & C Black, London, England, 1958. Schwiebert, Ernest.; *Trout*, E. P. Dutton, New York, New York, 1978.
- Skues, G.E.M.; *Minor Tactics of the Chalk Stream*, A & C Black, London, England, 1910.
- Skues, G.E.M.; *The Way of a Trout with a Fly*, A & C Black, London, England, 1921.
- Skues, G.E.M.; *Side Lines, Side Lights, and Reflections*, Seeley and Co., London, England, 1932.
- Skues, G.E.M.; *Nymph Fishing For Chalk Stream Trout*, A & C Black, London, England, 1939.
- Skues, G.E.M.; *Itchen Memories*, Hebert Jenkins, London, England, 1951.
- Stewart, W. C.; *The Practical Angler*, A & C Black, Edinburgh, Scotland 1857.
- Theakston, Michael.; *British Angling Flies*, William Harrison, London, England, 1883.

INDEX

Learn More About Fly-Fishing and Fly-Tying with These Popular Books!

THE BENCHSIDE INTRODUCTION TO FLY TYING
by Ted Leeson & Jim Schollmeyer

Renowned writing team Ted Leeson and Jim Schollmeyer have set another milestone in the world of fly tying with this unique new addition to their Benchside Reference series. Following the incredible success of *The Fly Tier's Benchside Reference*, Jim & Ted now offer the first beginner's book of fly tying to allow readers simultaneous access to fly recipes, tying steps, and techniques. No more flipping back and forth from fly pattern to technique, hoping the wings don't fall off your mayfly. The first 50 pages of this oversized, spiral-bound book are filled with impeccably photographed fly-tying techniques. The next 150 pages are cut horizontally across the page. The top pages show tying steps for dozens of fly patterns, including references to tying techniques that are explained step by step in the bottom pages. This groundbreaking book is sure to thrill all fly tiers. Over 1500 beautiful color photographs, 9 X 12 inches, 190 all-color pages.

SPIRAL HB: $45.00
ISBN: 1-57188-369-X UPC: 0-81127-00203-0

TYING EMERGERS
by Jim Schollmeyer and Ted Leeson

Two of fly-fishing's most well-respected writers collaborate once again, this time discussing emergers. Emergence is itself a behavior, and it puts the tier in a challenging and rather unusual position—not that of imitating a fixed and recognizable form of the insect, but rather of representing a process. This book shows you how, including: emerger design and materials, basic tying techniques, many specialized tying techniques, fly patterns, and more. When you buy a book by these two authors you know what you will get—up-to-the-minute information, well-written text, and superb photography, Tying Emergers will not let you down. 8 1/2 x 11 inches, 344 pages.

SB: $45.00
ISBN: 1-57188-306-1
UPC: 0-81127-00140-8

Spiral HB: $60.00
ISBN: 1-57188-307-X
UPC: 0-81127-00141-5

LTD. HB: $125.00
ISBN: 1-57188-320-7

FLY TYING MADE CLEAR AND SIMPLE
by Skip Morris

With over 220 color photographs, expert tier show all the techniques you need to know. 73 different materials and 27 tools. Clear, precise advice tells you how to do it step-by-step. Dries, wets, streamers, nymphs, etc., included so that you can tie virtually any pattern. 8 1/2 x 11 inches, 80 pages.

SPIRAL SB: $19.95
ISBN: 1-878175-13-0
UPC: 0-66066-00103-0

SB: $19.95
ISBN: 1-57188-231-6
UPC: 0-81127-00131-6

ROD-BUILDING GUIDE
Fly, Spinning, Casting, Trolling
by Tom Kirkman

Building your own rod is challenging, rewarding, and fun! This book will show you how. Tom covers: blanks and components; rod-building tools; adhesive and bonding techniques; understanding rod spine; grip, handle, and seat assembly; guide placement, guide prep and wrapping; finishing; and more. This is a book a beginner can understand and from which an old pro can learn some new techniques. Full color, 8 1/2 x 11 inches, 51 pages.

SB: $14.95
ISBN: 1-57188-216-2
UPC: 0-66066-00430-7

THE FLY TIER'S BENCHSIDE REFERENCE TO TECHNIQUES AND DRESSING STYLES
by Ted Leeson and Jim Schollmeyer

Printed in full color on top-quality paper, this book features over 3,000 color photographs and over 400,000 words describing and showing, step-by-step, hundreds of fly-tying techniques! Leeson and Schollmeyer have collaborated to produce this masterful volume which will be the standard fly-tying reference book for the entire trout-fishing world. Through enormous effort on their part they bring to all who love flies and fly fishing a wonderful compendium of fly-tying knowledge. Every fly tier should have this book in their library! All color, 8 1/2 by 11 inches, 464 pages, over 3,000 color photographs, index, hardbound with dust jacket.

HB: $100.00
ISBN: 1-57188-126-3
UPC: 0-81127-00107-1

NYMPH FLY-TYING TECHNIQUES
by Jim Schollmeyer

Noted photographer and author, Jim Schollmeyer, now puts his talents to tying nymphs. More than just a book of nymph patterns, this book takes a different approach. Realizing that many nymph patterns have evolved from variations on a handful of basic designs and tying techniques, Jim has written on these evolutions and how your repertoire of flies can be broadened by seeing how a variety of modifications can be worked into fly designs to produce the desired appearance or behavior.

With his crisp step-by-step photos and concise text, Jim Schollmeyer has done it again, another great fly-tying technique book. Full-color, 8 1/2 x 11 inches, 125 pages.

SB: $23.95
ISBN: 1-57188-266-9
UPC: 0-66066-00455-0

SPIRAL HB: $43.00
ISBN: 1-57188-267-7
UPC: 0-66066-00456-7

AMERICAN FLY TYING MANUAL
by Dave Hughes

Clear illustrations and photos (83) show you how to tie all 290 patterns in the book which are shown in full color and large size with tying instructions adjacent to each. Best-producing North American flies, including most popular dry, nymph, wet, streamer and bucktail, steelhead, Atlantic salmon, Pacific salmon, cutthroat, Alaskan, saltwater, bass, and panfish patterns. Color plates of tying materials, including fur, hackle, thread, etc. Fly pattern index. Fishing tips for most patterns. Printed on heavy, gloss paper stock. Bound for easy opening. 8 1/2 x 11 inches, 48 pages.

SB: $9.95
ISBN: 1-57188-212-X
UPC: 0-66066-00426-0

HATCH GUIDE FOR NEW ENGLAND STREAMS
by Thomas Ames, Jr.

New England's streams, and the insects and fish that inhabit them, have their own unique qualities that support an amazing diversity of insect species from all of the major orders. This book covers: reading water; presentations for New England streams; tackle; night fishing; and more. Ames discusses the natural and its behaviors and the three best flies to imitate it, including proper size and effective techniques. Tom's color photography of the naturals and their imitations is superb! Full color. 4 x 4 inches, 272 pages; insect and fly plates.

SB: $19.95
ISBN: 1-57188-210-3
UPC: 0-66066-00424-6

MAYFLIES: TOP TO BOTTOM
by Shane Stalcup

Shane Stalcup approaches fly-tying with the heart and mind of both a scientist and an artist. His realistic approach to imitating the mayfly is very popular and effective across the West, and can be applied to waters across North America. Mayflies are the most important insects to trout fishermen, and in this book, Shane shares his secrets for tying effective, lifelike mayfly imitations that will bring fly-anglers more trout. Many tying techniques and materials are discussed, *Mayflies: Top to Bottom* is useful to beginner and expert tiers alike. 8 1/2 x 11 inches, 157 pages.

SB: $29.95
ISBN: 1-57188-242-1
UPC: 0-66066-00496-3

Spiral HB: $39.95
ISBN: 1-57188-243-X
UPC: 0-81127-00116-3

FLY PATTERNS FOR STILLWATERS
by Philip Rowley

Phil has spent countless hours at lakes studying the food sources that make up the diet of trout; then set up home aquariums to more closely observe the movement, development, and emergence of the aquatic insects. In this book he explains the link between understanding the food base within lakes to designing effective fly patterns for these environs. Phil covers all major trout food sources for the whole year. He gives detailed information on each, plus how to tie a representative pattern and fish it effectively. Numerous proven stillwater patterns are given for each insect and include clear and concise tying instructions. All-color, 8 1/2 x 11 inches, 104 pages.

SB: $29.95
ISBN: 1-57188-195-6
UPC: 0-66066-00406-2

CURTIS CREEK MANIFESTO
by Sheridan Anderson

Finest beginner fly-fishing guide due to its simple, straightforward approach. It is laced with outstanding humor provided in its hundreds of illustrations. All the practical information you need to know is presented in an extremely delightful way such as rod, reel, fly line and fly selection, casting, reading water, insect knowledge to determine which fly pattern to use, striking and playing fish, leaders and knot tying, fly tying, rod repairs, and many helpful tips. A great, easy-to-understand book. 8 1/2 x 11 inches, 48 pages.

SB: $7.95
ISBN: 0-936608-06-4
UPC: 0-81127-00113-2

HATCH GUIDE FOR WESTERN STREAMS
by Jim Schollmeyer

Successful fishing on Western streams requires preparation—you need to know what insects are emerging, when and where, and which patterns best match them. Now, thanks to Jim Schollmeyer, the guessing is over.

Hatch Guide for Western Streams is the third in Jim's successful "Hatch Guide" series. Jim covers all you need for a productive trip on Western streams: water types you'll encounter; successful fishing techniques; identifying the major hatches, providing basic background information about these insects. Information is presented in a simple, clear manner. A full-color photograph of the natural is shown on the left-hand page, complete with its characteristics, habits and habitat; the right-hand page shows three flies to match the natural, including effective fishing techniques. 4 x 5 inches, full-color; 196 pages; fantastic photographs of naturals and flies.

SB: $19.95
ISBN: 1-57188-109-3
UPC: 0-66066-00303-4

Ask for these books at your local fly shop or book store, if unavailable call 1-800-541-9498 and order direct. We also offer hundreds of other fly-tying and fly-fishing titles on our website www.amatobooks.com